1 & 2 Peter
1, 2, & 3 John
Jude

ABOUT THE AUTHORS

General editor:

Clinton E. Arnold (PhD, University of Aberdeen), professor and chairman, department of New Testament, Talbot School of Theology, Biola University, Los Angeles, California

1 Peter:

Peter H. Davids (PhD, University of Manchester), adjunct professor of New Testament/educational missionary, Tyndale Theological Seminary, Amsterdam, the Netherlands, and International Teams, Innsbruck, Austria

2 Peter:

Douglas J. Moo (PhD, University of St. Andrews), Blanchard professor of New Testament, Wheaton College Graduate School, Wheaton, Illinois

1, 2, 3 John:

Robert W. Yarbrough (PhD, University of Aberdeen), associate professor of New Testament and department chair, Trinity Evangelical Divinity School, Trinity International University, Deerfield, Illinois

Jude:

Douglas J. Moo (PhD, University of St. Andrews), Blanchard professor of New Testament, Wheaton College Graduate School, Wheaton, Illinois

Zondervan Illustrated Bible Backgrounds Commentary

1 & 2 Peter
1, 2, & 3 John
Jude

Peter H. Davids

Douglas J. Moo

Robert W. Yarbrough

Clinton E. Arnold *general editor*

ZONDERVAN®

ZONDERVAN.com/
AUTHORTRACKER
follow your favorite authors

ZONDERVAN®

Zondervan Illustrated Bible Backgrounds Commentary

Requests for information should be addressed to:

Zondervan, *Grand Rapids, Michigan 49530*

Library of Congress Cataloging-in-Publication Data

Zondervan illustrated Bible backgrounds commentary / Clinton E. Arnold, general editor.
p.cm.
Includes bibliographical references.
ISBN-10: 0-310-27824-4
ISBN-13: 978-0-310-27824-5
1. Bible. N.T.—Commentaries. I. Arnold, Clinton E.
BS2341.52.Z66 2001
225.7—dc21 2001046801
CIP

Printed in China

Interior design by Sherri L. Hoffman

07 08 09 10 11 12 13 • 12 11 10 9 8 7 6 5 4 3 2 1

CONTENTS

INTRODUCTION

All readers of the Bible have a tendency to view what it says it through their own culture and life circumstances. This can happen almost subconsiously as we read the pages of the text.

When most people in the church read about the thief on the cross, for instance, they immediately think of a burglar that held up a store or broke into a home. They may be rather shocked to find out that the guy was actually a Jewish revolutionary figure who was part of a growing movement in Palestine eager to throw off Roman rule.

It also comes as something of a surprise to contemporary Christians that "cursing" in the New Testament era had little or nothing to do with cussing somebody out. It had far more to do with the invocation of spirits to cause someone harm.

No doubt there is a need in the church for learning more about the world of the New Testament to avoid erroneous interpretations of the text of Scripture. But relevant historical and cultural insights also provide an added dimension of perspective to the words of the Bible. This kind of information often functions in the same way as watching a movie in color rather than in black and white. Finding out, for instance, how Paul compared Christ's victory on the cross to a joyous celebration parade in honor of a Roman general after winning an extraordinary battle brings does indeed magnify the profundity and implications of Jesus' work on the cross. Discovering that the factions at Corinth ("I follow Paul . . . I follow Apollos . . .") had plenty of precedent in the local cults ("I follow Aphrodite; I follow Apollo . . .") helps us understand the "why" of a particular problem. Learning about the water supply from the springs of Hierapolis that flowed into Laodicea as "lukewarm" water enables us to appreciate the relevance of the metaphor Jesus used when he addressed the spiritual laxity of this church.

My sense is that most Christians are eager to learn more about the real life setting of the New Testament. In the preaching and teaching of the Bible in the church, congregants are always grateful when they learn something of the background and historical context of the text. It not only helps them understand the text more accurately, but often enables them to identify with the people and circumstances of the Bible. I have been asked on countless occasions by Christians, "Where can I get access to good historical background information about this passage?" Earnest Christians are hungry for information that makes their Bibles come alive.

The stimulus for this commentary came from the church and the aim is to serve the church. The contributors to this series have sought to provide illuminating and interesting historical/cultural background information. The intent was to draw upon relevant papyri, inscriptions, archaeological discoveries, and the numerous studies of Judaism, Roman culture, Hellenism, and other features of the world of the New Testament and to make the results accessible to people in the church. We recognize that some readers of the commentary will want to go further, and so the sources of the information have been carefully documented in endnotes.

The written information has been supplemented with hundreds of photographs, maps, charts, artwork, and other graphics that help the reader better understand the world of the New Testament. Each of the writers was given an opportunity to dream up a "wish list" of illustrations that he thought would help to illustrate the passages in the New Testament book for which he was writing commentary. Although we were not able to obtain everything they were looking for, we came close.

The team of commentators are writing for the benefit of the broad array of Christians who simply want to better understand their Bibles from the vantage point of the historical context. This is an installment in a new genre of "Bible background" commentaries that was kicked off by Craig Keener's fine volume. Consequently, this is not an "exegetical" commentary that provides linguistic insight and background into Greek constructions and verb tenses. Neither is this work an "expository" commentary that provides a verse-by-verse exposition of the text; for in-depth philological or theological insight, readers will need to have other more specialized or comprehensive commentaries available. Nor is this an "historical-critical" commentary, although the contributors are all scholars and have already made substantial academic contributions on the New Testament books they are writing on for this set. The team intentionally does not engage all of the issues that are discussed in the scholarly guild.

Rather, our goal is to offer a reading and interpretation of the text informed by what we regard as the most relevant historical information. For many in the church, this commentary will serve as an important entry point into the interpretation and appreciation of the text. For other more serious students of the Word, these volumes will provide an important supplement to many of the fine exegetical, expository, and critical available.

The contributors represent a group of scholars who embrace the Bible as the Word of God and believe that the message of its pages has life-changing relevance for faith and practice today. Accordingly, we offer "Reflections" on the relevance of the Scripture to life for every chapter of the New Testament.

I pray that this commentary brings you both delight and insight in digging deeper into the Word of God.

Clinton E. Arnold
General Editor

LIST OF SIDEBARS

1 Peter

2 Peter

1 John

2 John

3 John

Jude

LIST OF CHARTS

INDEX OF PHOTOS AND MAPS

ABBREVIATIONS

1. Books of the Bible and Apocrypha

1 Chron.	1 Chronicles
2 Chron.	2 Chronicles
1 Cor.	1 Corinthians
2 Cor.	2 Corinthians
1 Esd.	1 Esdras
2 Esd.	2 Esdras
1 John	1 John
2 John	2 John
3 John	3 John
1 Kings	1 Kings
2 Kings	2 Kings
1 Macc.	1 Maccabees
2 Macc.	2 Maccabees
1 Peter	1 Peter
2 Peter	2 Peter
1 Sam.	1 Samuel
2 Sam.	2 Samuel
1 Thess.	1 Thessalonians
2 Thess.	2 Thessalonians
1 Tim.	1 Timothy
2 Tim.	2 Timothy
Acts	Acts
Amos	Amos
Bar.	Baruch
Bel	Bel and the Dragon
Col.	Colossians
Dan.	Daniel
Deut.	Deuteronomy
Eccl.	Ecclesiastes
Ep. Jer.	Epistle of Jeremiah
Eph.	Ephesians
Est.	Esther
Ezek.	Ezekiel
Ex.	Exodus
Ezra	Ezra
Gal.	Galatians
Gen.	Genesis
Hab.	Habakkuk
Hag.	Haggai
Heb.	Hebrews
Hos.	Hosea
Isa.	Isaiah
James	James
Jer.	Jeremiah
Job	Job
Joel	Joel
John	John
Jonah	Jonah
Josh.	Joshua
Jude	Jude
Judg.	Judges
Judith	Judith
Lam.	Lamentations
Lev.	Leviticus
Luke	Luke
Mal.	Malachi
Mark	Mark
Matt.	Matthew
Mic.	Micah
Nah.	Nahum
Neh.	Nehemiah
Num.	Numbers
Obad.	Obadiah
Phil.	Philippians
Philem.	Philemon
Pr. Man.	Prayer of Manassah
Prov.	Proverbs
Ps.	Psalm
Rest. of Est.	The Rest of Esther
Rev.	Revelation
Rom.	Romans
Ruth	Ruth
S. of III Ch.	The Song of the Three Holy Children
Sir.	Sirach/Ecclesiasticus
Song	Song of Songs
Sus.	Susanna
Titus	Titus
Tobit	Tobit
Wisd. Sol.	The Wisdom of Solomon
Zech.	Zechariah
Zeph.	Zephaniah

2. Old and New Testament Pseudepigrapha and Rabbinic Literature

Individual tractates of rabbinic literature follow the abbreviations of the *SBL Handbook of Style*, pp. 79–80. Qumran documents follow standard Dead Sea Scroll conventions.

2 Bar.	*2 Baruch*
3 Bar.	*3 Baruch*
4 Bar.	*4 Baruch*
1 En.	*1 Enoch*
2 En.	*2 Enoch*
3 En.	*3 Enoch*
4 Ezra	*4 Ezra*

3 Macc.	*3 Maccabees*
4 Macc.	*4 Maccabees*
5 Macc.	*5 Maccabees*
Acts Phil.	*Acts of Philip*
Acts Pet.	*Acts of Peter and the 12 Apostles*
Apoc. Elijah	*Apocalypse of Elijah*
As. Mos.	*Assumption of Moses*
b.	*Babylonian Talmud* (+ tractate)
Gos. Thom.	*Gospel of Thomas*
Jos. Asen.	*Joseph and Aseneth*
Jub.	*Jubilees*
Let. Aris.	*Letter of Aristeas*
m.	*Mishnah* (+ tractate)
Mek.	*Mekilta*
Midr.	*Midrash I* (+ biblical book)
Odes Sol.	*Odes of Solomon*
Pesiq. Rab.	*Pesiqta Rabbati*
Pirqe. R. El.	*Pirqe Rabbi Eliezer*
Pss. Sol.	*Psalms of Solomon*
Rab.	*Rabbah* (+biblical book); (e.g., *Gen. Rab.=Genesis Rabbah)*
S. ʿOlam Rab.	*Seder ʿOlam Rabbah*
Sem.	*Semahot*
Sib. Or.	*Sibylline Oracles*
T. Ab.	*Testament of Abraham*
T. Adam	*Testament of Adam*
T. Ash.	*Testament of Asher*
T. Benj.	*Testament of Benjamin*
T. Dan	*Testament of Dan*
T. Gad	*Testament of Gad*
T. Hez.	*Testament of Hezekiah*
T. Isaac	*Testament of Isaac*
T. Iss.	*Testament of Issachar*
T. Jac.	*Testament of Jacob*
T. Job	*Testament of Job*
T. Jos.	*Testament of Joseph*
T. Jud.	*Testament of Judah*
T. Levi	*Testament of Levi*
T. Mos.	*Testament of Moses*
T. Naph.	*Testament of Naphtali*
T. Reu.	*Testament of Reuben*
T. Sim.	*Testament of Simeon*
T. Sol.	*Testament of Solomon*
T. Zeb.	*Testament of Zebulum*
Tanh.	*Tanhuma*
Tg. Isa.	*Targum of Isaiah*
Tg. Lam.	*Targum of Lamentations*
Tg. Neof.	*Targum Neofiti*
Tg. Onq.	*Targum Onqelos*
Tg. Ps.-J	*Targum Pseudo-Jonathan*
y.	*Jerusalem Talmud* (+ tractate)

3. Classical Historians

For an extended list of classical historians and church fathers, see *SBL Handbook of Style*, pp. 84–87. For many works of classical antiquity, the abbreviations have been subjected to the author's discretion; the names of these works should be obvious upon consulting entries of the classical writers in classical dictionaries or encyclopedias.

Eusebius

Eccl. Hist.	*Ecclesiastical History*

Josephus

Ag. Ap.	*Against Apion*
Ant.	*Jewish Antiquities*
J.W.	*Jewish War*
Life	*The Life*

Philo

Abraham	On the Life of Abraham
Agriculture	On Agriculture
Alleg. Interp	*Allegorical Interpretation*
Animals	*Whether Animals Have Reason*
Cherubim	*On the Cherubim*
Confusion	*On the Confusion of Thomas*
Contempl. Life	*On the Contemplative Life*
Creation	*On the Creation of the World*
Curses	*On Curses*
Decalogue	*On the Decalogue*
Dreams	*On Dreams*
Drunkenness	*On Drunkenness*
Embassy	*On the Embassy to Gaius*
Eternity	*On the Eternity of the World*
Flaccus	*Against Flaccus*
Flight	*On Flight and Finding*
Giants	*On Giants*
God	*On God*
Heir	*Who Is the Heir?*
Hypothetica	*Hypothetica*
Joseph	*On the Life of Joseph*
Migration	*On the Migration of Abraham*
Moses	*On the Life of Moses*
Names	*On the Change of Names*
Person	*That Every Good Person Is Free*
Planting	*On Planting*
Posterity	*On the Posterity of Cain*
Prelim. Studies	*On the Preliminary Studies*
Providence	*On Providence*
QE	*Questions and Answers on Exodus*
QG	*Questions and Answers on Genesis*
Rewards	*On Rewards and Punishments*
Sacrifices	*On the Sacrifices of Cain and Abel*
Sobriety	*On Sobriety*
Spec. Laws	*On the Special Laws*
Unchangeable	*That God Is Unchangeable*
Virtues	*On the Virtues*
Worse	*That the Worse Attacks the Better*

Apostolic Fathers

1 Clem.	*First Letter of Clement*
Barn.	*Epistle of Barnabas*
Clem. Hom.	*Ancient Homily of Clement* (also called *2 Clement)*
Did.	*Didache*
Herm. Vis.; Sim.	*Shepherd of Hermas, Visions; Similitudes*
Ignatius	*Epistles of Ignatius* (followed by the letter's name)
Mart. Pol.	*Martyrdom of Polycarp*

4. Modern Abbreviations

AASOR	Annual of the American Schools of Oriental Research
AB	Anchor Bible
ABD	*Anchor Bible Dictionary*
ABRL	Anchor Bible Reference Library
AGJU	Arbeiten zur Geschichte des antiken Judentums und des Urchristentums
AH	*Agricultural History*
ALGHJ	Arbeiten zur Literatur und Geschichte des Hellenistischen Judentums
AnBib	Analecta biblica
ANRW	*Aufstieg und Niedergang der römischen Welt*
ANTC	Abingdon New Testament Commentaries
BAGD	Bauer, W., W. F. Arndt, F. W. Gingrich, and F. W. Danker. *Greek-English Lexicon of the New Testament and Other Early Christina Literature* (2d. ed.)
BA	*Biblical Archaeologist*
BAFCS	Book of Acts in Its First Century Setting
BAR	*Biblical Archaeology Review*
BASOR	*Bulletin of the American Schools of Oriental Research*
BBC	*Bible Background Commentary*
BBR	*Bulletin for Biblical Research*
BDB	Brown, F., S. R. Driver, and C. A. Briggs. *A Hebrew and English Lexicon of the Old Testament*
BDF	Blass, F., A. Debrunner, and R. W. Funk. *A Greek Grammar of the New Testament and Other Early Christian Literature*
BECNT	Baker Exegetical Commentary on the New Testament
BI	*Biblical Illustrator*
Bib	*Biblica*
BibSac	*Bibliotheca Sacra*
BLT	Brethren Life and Thought
BNTC	Black's New Testament Commentary
BRev	*Bible Review*
BSHJ	Baltimore Studies in the History of Judaism
BST	The Bible Speaks Today
BSV	Biblical Social Values
BT	*The Bible Translator*
BTB	*Biblical Theology Bulletin*
BZ	*Biblische Zeitschrift*
CBQ	*Catholic Biblical Quarterly*
CBTJ	*Calvary Baptist Theological Journal*
CGTC	Cambridge Greek Testament Commentary
CH	*Church History*
CIL	*Corpus inscriptionum latinarum*
CPJ	*Corpus papyrorum judaicorum*
CRINT	*Compendia rerum iudaicarum ad Novum Testamentum*
CTJ	*Calvin Theological Journal*
CTM	*Concordia Theological Monthly*
CTT	Contours of Christian Theology
DBI	*Dictionary of Biblical Imagery*
DCM	*Dictionary of Classical Mythology.*
DDD	*Dictionary of Deities and Demons in the Bible*
DJBP	*Dictionary of Judaism in the Biblical Period*
DJG	*Dictionary of Jesus and the Gospels*
DLNT	*Dictionary of the Later New Testament and Its Developments*
DNTB	*Dictionary of New Testament Background*
DPL	*Dictionary of Paul and His Letters*
EBC	*Expositor's Bible Commentary*
EDBT	*Evangelical Dictionary of Biblical Theology*
EDNT	*Exegetical Dictionary of the New Testament*
EJR	*Encyclopedia of the Jewish Religion*
EPRO	Études préliminaires aux religions orientales dans l'empire romain
EvQ	*Evangelical Quarterly*
ExpTim	*Expository Times*
FRLANT	Forsuchungen zur Religion und Literatur des Alten und Neuen Testament
GNC	Good News Commentary
GNS	Good News Studies
HCNT	*Hellenistic Commentary to the New Testament*
HDB	*Hastings Dictionary of the Bible*
HJP	*History of the Jewish People in the Age of Jesus Christ*, by E. Schürer

HTR	*Harvard Theological Review*
HTS	Harvard Theological Studies
HUCA	*Hebrew Union College Annual*
IBD	*Illustrated Bible Dictionary*
IBS	*Irish Biblical Studies*
ICC	International Critical Commentary
IDB	*The Interpreter's Dictionary of the Bible*
IEJ	*Israel Exploration Journal*
IG	*Inscriptiones graecae*
IGRR	*Inscriptiones graecae ad res romanas pertinentes*
ILS	*Inscriptiones Latinae Selectae*
Imm	*Immanuel*
ISBE	*International Standard Bible Encyclopedia*
Int	*Interpretation*
IvE	*Inschriften von Ephesos*
IVPNTC	InterVarsity Press New Testament Commentary
JAC	*Jahrbuch fur Antike und Christentum*
JBL	*Journal of Biblical Literature*
JETS	*Journal of the Evangelical Theological Society*
JHS	*Journal of Hellenic Studies*
JJS	*Journal of Jewish Studies*
JOAIW	*Jahreshefte des Osterreeichischen Archaologischen Instites in Wien*
JSJ	*Journal for the Study of Judaism in the Persian, Hellenistic, and Roman Periods*
JRS	*Journal of Roman Studies*
JSNT	*Journal for the Study of the New Testament*
JSNTSup	Journal for the Study of the New Testament: Supplement Series
JSOT	*Journal for the Study of the Old Testament*
JSOTSup	Journal for the Study of the Old Testament: Supplement Series
JTS	*Journal of Theological Studies*
KTR	*Kings Theological Review*
LCL	Loeb Classical Library
LEC	Library of Early Christianity
LSJ	Liddell, H. G., R. Scott, H. S. Jones. *A Greek-English Lexicon*
MM	Moulton, J. H., and G. Milligan. *The Vocabulary of the Greek Testament*
MNTC	Moffatt New Testament Commentary
NBD	*New Bible Dictionary*
NC	Narrative Commentaries
NCBC	New Century Bible Commentary Eerdmans
NEAE	*New Encyclopedia of Archaeological Excavations in the Holy Land*
NEASB	*Near East Archaeological Society Bulletin*
New Docs	*New Documents Illustrating Early Christianity*
NIBC	New International Biblical Commentary
NICNT	New International Commentary on the New Testament
NIDNTT	*New International Dictionary of New Testament Theology*
NIGTC	New International Greek Testament Commentary
NIVAC	NIV Application Commentary
NorTT	*Norsk Teologisk Tidsskrift*
NoT	*Notes on Translation*
NovT	*Novum Testamentum*
NovTSup	Novum Testamentum Supplements
NTAbh	Neutestamentliche Abhandlungen
NTS	*New Testament Studies*
NTT	New Testament Theology
NTTS	New Testament Tools and Studies
OAG	Oxford Archaeological Guides
OCCC	Oxford Companion to Classical Civilization
OCD	Oxford Classical Dictionary
ODCC	The Oxford Dictionary of the Christian Church
OGIS	Orientis graeci inscriptiones selectae
OHCW	The Oxford History of the Classical World
OHRW	Oxford History of the Roman World
OTP	Old Testament Pseudepigrapha, ed. by J. H. Charlesworth
PEQ	*Palestine Exploration Quarterly*
PG	*Patrologia graeca*
PGM	*Papyri graecae magicae: Die griechischen Zauberpapyri*
PL	*Patrologia latina*
PNTC	Pelican New Testament Commentaries
Rb	*Revista biblica*
RB	*Revue biblique*
RivB	*Rivista biblica italiana*
RTR	*Reformed Theological Review*
SB	Sources bibliques
SBL	Society of Biblical Literature
SBLDS	Society of Biblical Literature Dissertation Series
SBLMS	Society of Biblical Literature Monograph Series

SBLSP	*Society of Biblical Literature Seminar Papers*
SBS	Stuttgarter Bibelstudien
SBT	Studies in Biblical Theology
SCJ	*Stone-Campbell Journal*
Scr	*Scripture*
SE	*Studia Evangelica*
SEG	*Supplementum epigraphicum graecum*
SJLA	Studies in Judaism in Late Antiquity
SJT	*Scottish Journal of Theology*
SNTSMS	Society for New Testament Studies Monograph Series
SSC	Social Science Commentary
SSCSSG	Social-Science Commentary on the Synoptic Gospels
Str-B	Strack, H. L., and P. Billerbeck. *Kommentar zum Neuen Testament aus Talmud und Midrasch*
TC	Thornapple Commentaries
TDNT	*Theological Dictionary of the New Testament*
TDOT	*Theological Dictionary of the Old Testament*
TLNT	*Theological Lexicon of the New Testament*
TLZ	*Theologische Literaturzeitung*
TNTC	Tyndale New Testament Commentary
TrinJ	*Trinity Journal*
TS	*Theological Studies*
TSAJ	Texte und Studien zum antiken Judentum
TWNT	*Theologische Wörterbuch zum Neuen Testament*
TynBul	*Tyndale Bulletin*
WBC	Word Biblical Commentary Waco: Word, 1982
WMANT	Wissenschaftliche Monographien zum Alten und Neuen Testament
WUNT	Wissenschaftliche Untersuchungen zum Neuen Testament
YJS	Yale Judaica Series
ZNW	*Zeitschrift fur die neutestamentliche Wissenschaft und die Junde der alteren Kirche*
ZPE	*Zeischrift der Papyrolgie und Epigraphkik*
ZPEB	*Zondervan Pictorial Encyclopedia of the Bible*

5. General Abbreviations

ad. loc.	in the place cited
b.	born
c., ca.	circa
cf.	compare
d.	died
ed(s).	editors(s), edited by
e.g.	for example
ET	English translation
frg.	fragment
i.e.	that is
ibid.	in the same place
idem	the same (author)
lit.	literally
l(l)	line(s)
MSS	manuscripts
n.d.	no date
NS	New Series
par.	parallel
passim	here and there
repr.	reprint
ser.	series
s.v.	*sub verbo*, under the word
trans.	translator, translated by; transitive

Zondervan Illustrated Bible Backgrounds Commentary

1 PETER

by Peter Davids

The Church in Northwest Asia Minor

We do not know when the church started in northwest Asia Minor. Paul planted churches in the southern Galatian region in the late A.D. 40s (Acts 13–14), but when he later tried to extend this work westward into Asia or northwestward into Bithynia, the Spirit prohibited him (16:6–7), apparently because the Lord wanted to use Paul in Macedonia and Achaia (Greece; 16:10). Paul's interest in those areas probably means that he did not know of churches there, for his general procedure was to go where the church did not yet exist (Rom. 15:20; 2 Cor. 10:14). Did the Lord know that some of the people cited in Acts 2:9 had already carried the gospel there, or was it his plan to leave the evangelization of that area to someone else at a later date? What we do know is that about fifteen years later

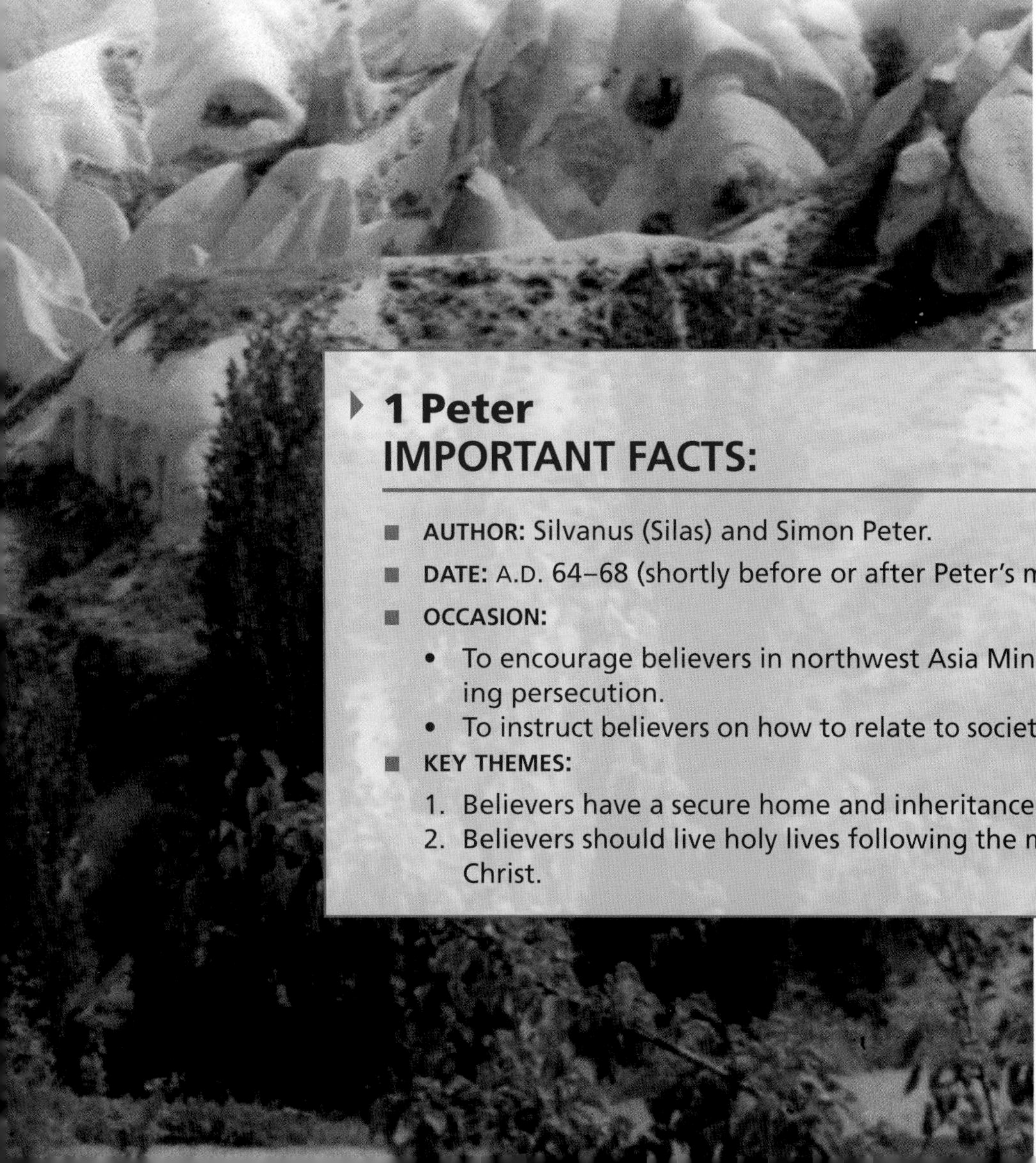

CAPPADOCIAN LANDSCAPE

1 Peter IMPORTANT FACTS:

- **AUTHOR:** Silvanus (Silas) and Simon Peter.
- **DATE:** A.D. 64–68 (shortly before or after Peter's martyrdom).
- **OCCASION:**
  - To encourage believers in northwest Asia Minor experiencing persecution.
  - To instruct believers on how to relate to societal structures.
- **KEY THEMES:**
  1. Believers have a secure home and inheritance with Christ.
  2. Believers should live holy lives following the model of Christ.

1 Peter witnesses to the existence of churches throughout this area. We should probably think of house churches scattered throughout the area, the larger ones consisting of thirty to forty members—sometimes several in one city (collectively forming the church in that city) and sometimes only one. They would be loosely connected as Christians traveled through the area for one reason or another, bringing news about other Christian groups as they went.

One thing that we do know about the churches of this area is that they were largely Gentile in makeup. First Peter frequently refers to these Christians in terms that would not be appropriate for Jews.[1] There is also none of the Jew-Gentile or circumcision-uncircumcision tension in this letter that is so common in Paul's writings. While Jews probably lived in these areas, as Acts 2:9 indicates, most of the church came from people native to the region. This made rejection by their neighbors as a result of their commitment to Christ so much more painful, since they had gone from being completely at home in the culture to being social outcasts.

Despite the problems mentioned in 1 Peter, these churches survived. When Trajan sent Pliny to Bithynia as Senatorial governor about A.D. 112, Pliny discovered, as he wrote to Trajan, "The contagion of that superstition [i.e., Christianity] has penetrated not the cities only, but the villages and the country."[2] Pliny himself thought he could still stamp Christianity out, but he would fail and the area would remain a strong Christian center for centuries.

ITALY

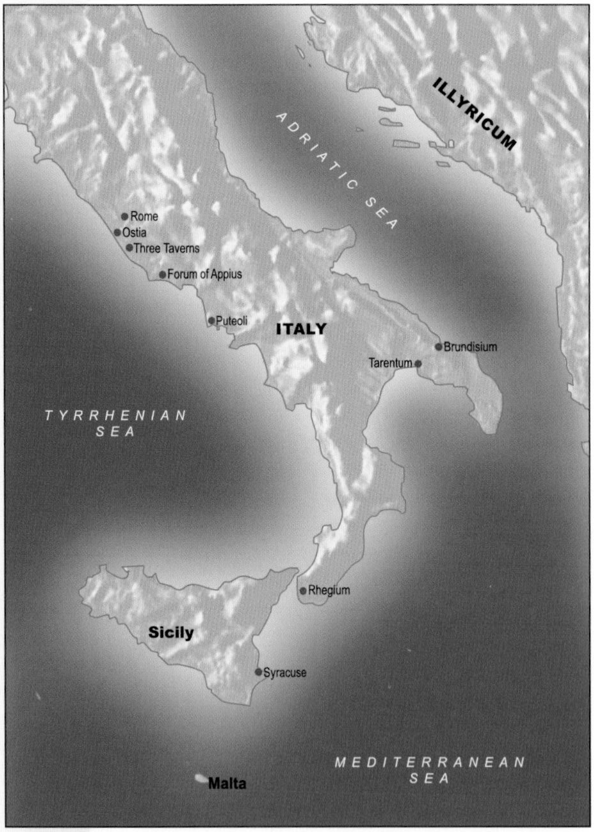

A Portrait of the Situation

When missionaries arrived in these provinces, people listened to the gospel and believed. As a result their lifestyle changed. First and foremost, they stopped worshiping the various gods of their empire, city, trade guild, or family, and instead worshiped only "the God and Father of our Lord Jesus Christ" (1:3). This change in behavior meant that they were now viewed as unpatriotic (worship of the genius of the emperor was equivalent to flag worship in modern America), disloyal to their city (since they would not take part in civic ceremonies involving worship), unprofessional in their trade (since guild meetings usually took place in pagan temples), and haters of their families (family gatherings and ceremonies also took place in temples, and household worship was thought to hold the family together). After all, no one was asking these Christians to believe in the gods (many of their neighbors did not really believe in them), but only to offer token worship as a sign of their familial or civic allegiance. People who were so obstinate as to refuse this simple duty surely had to be "haters of humankind," as many in the Roman Empire considered them.

Second, they now followed a morality different from that of their fellow citizens. Previously they had enjoyed drunken parties and loose sexual morals, but now they demonstrated self-control in their drinking, eating, and sexual habits. This different behavior cut them off from their former friends, who thought that they had become weird (4:4).

The result of these changes in their lives was social ostracism: insults, abuse, rejection, shame, and likely economic persecution with the resulting loss of property. There is no evidence in this letter of official persecution, such as imprisonment or execution, but rejection, abuse, punishment by family leaders (owners of slaves; husbands of women) and perhaps occasional mob violence had certainly taken their toll. (Official persecution would come in the time of Pliny.) Their fellow citizens thought that these believers in Jesus no longer belonged in their city or family and were communicating that message loud and clear.

This is the situation that has come to the attention of our writer. He apparently does not know these Christians personally (the letter lacks the personal greetings found in many of Paul's letters), but he is concerned about their situation. He will write to them, citing the general Christian teachings he is sure they know. He follows a threefold strategy in his letter: (1) to exhort them to stand firm in the light of the return of Christ, (2) to advise them on how to minimize persecution through wise behavior, and (3) to encourage them to consider where they do belong and what property they do own because they belong to Christ.

CITY GATE AT NICEA, BITHYNIA

These strategies should be kept in mind as one reads the letter.

Letter Opening (1:1–2)

Peter, an apostle of Jesus Christ (1:1). It was standard practice in the ancient world to begin a letter by identifying the sender. Normally the sender was viewed as the person who either dictated the letter or requested someone to write it for him, not the secretary who wrote down the dictated words or, if trusted, composed the letter on behalf of the sender. Our letter is from Peter (meaning "Rock"), and since that was a common name, he identifies which Peter is writing, namely, the one who was sent or commissioned (the meaning of "apostle") by Jesus Christ.

To God's elect, strangers in the world, scattered throughout Pontus, Galatia, Cappadocia, Asia and Bithynia (1:1). After identifying the sender, ancient letters identified the recipients. Peter is sensitive to the situation of his readers. Their society may reject them, but they are chosen (elect) by God (which idea is underlined in the next verse). They may be technically citizens of their various cities, but the way their fellow citizens treat them and the reality of their new life in Christ make them feel like temporary residents, noncitizens (both better translations than "strangers"). We will later discover where they really belong. At present they are scattered, which term would remind any Jews among them of the scattering of the Jewish people among the nations (called the "Diaspora," a word from the same root as the term "scattered") at the time of the Exile (586 B.C.) and the hope of their eventual regathering in Palestine.

The sanctifying work of the Spirit, for obedience to Jesus Christ and sprinkling by his blood (1:2). The idea that the Spirit sanctifies indicates not simply a positional change when God reached out to them, but a practical change in lifestyle for the better, from a less holy lifestyle to one that is set apart for God. This change appeared in their obedience to Jesus Christ. The basic Christian confession was "Jesus is Lord," which contrasted with the assertion of the Roman

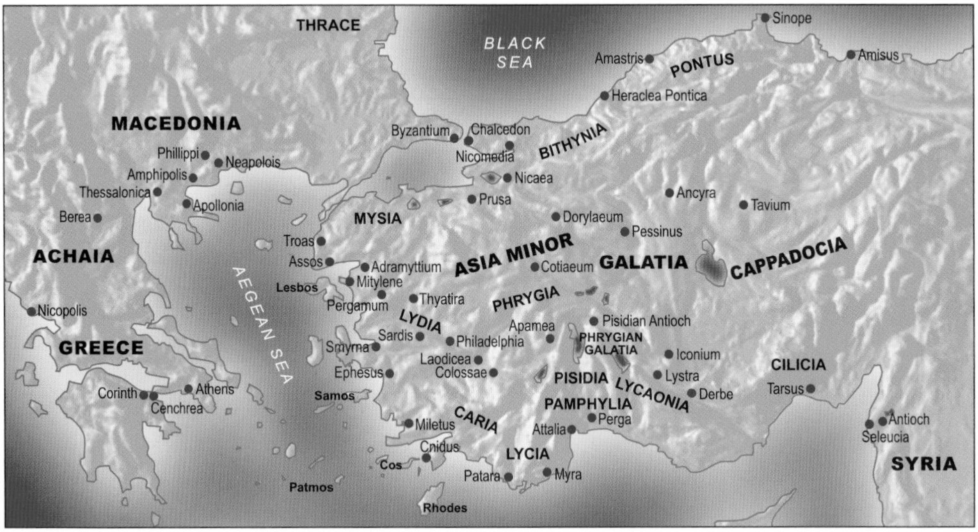

ASIA MINOR

Empire that "Caesar is Lord." In both cases "Lord" implied that the person was someone whom you obeyed. It had practical consequences. This clash in allegiance was one cause of the persecution of the church. In chapter 2, Peter will set this clash of allegiance in perspective.

The image of sprinkling is taken from Old Testament and pagan sacrificial rites, with which the readers were surely familiar. They had all seen animals sacrificed and the blood sprinkled on people or objects for various religious purposes. Peter is probably thinking primarily of the Old Testament. For example, in Exodus 24:7–8 we read that the people respond to the law (which began with announcing God's choice of them to be his people) with obedience, "We will do everything the LORD has said; we will obey." As a result, "Moses . . . took the blood, sprinkled it on the people and said, 'This is the blood of the covenant that the LORD has made with you in accordance with all these words.'" The sprinkled blood sealed the covenant and set the people apart for God.

Grace and peace be yours in abundance (1:2). A Greek letter normally had a greeting. In Christian letters this normal greeting (*chairein,* which in Greek sounds like the word for "grace," *charin,* and so was changed to "grace") was expanded with the Hebrew greeting (*shalom* = peace). However, it still retained its character as a formal greeting and thus functions like the "dear" that is often found at the beginning of English letters.

Thanksgiving 1:3–12

Praise be to the God and Father of our Lord Jesus Christ! (1:3). A normal Greek letter followed the greeting with thanks to one or more of the gods for the benefits that had been given to the letter writer or recipients. Christians tended to expand this rather short, formal thanksgiving into a much longer statement that often introduced some of the significant theological themes of the letter. Peter is no exception to that practice. Naturally, the God he praises is "the God and Father of our Lord Jesus Christ," which fits the New Testament tendency to worship the Father much more than Jesus.

In his great mercy he has given us new birth into a living hope (1:3). Christians were not the only ones who could talk about a new birth. In some of the pagan mystery religions[3] (e.g., Mithraism) one

BITHYNIA

Part of the ornamentation on the city gate at Nicea.

went through initiatory experiences that led to new life or new birth or life on a higher order. Despite the possibility of confusion with pagan beliefs, Peter (like John) prefers birth imagery rather than Paul's usual choice of adoption imagery for describing new life in Christ. The contrast with pagan belief is clear, however. While pagan religion brought about rebirth through instruction and various rites, that is, human activities, the Christian's rebirth had come through the activity of another person, "through the resurrection of Jesus Christ from the dead." The emphasis of the sentence is that of "a living hope," which both fits with the birth imagery and contrasts with the somewhat hopeless situation believers were physically living in.

An inheritance that can never perish, spoil or fade—kept in heaven for you (1:4). The hope is defined in terms of an inheritance. In the Old Testament Abraham was promised an inheritance (Gen. 12:7), which was the land of Canaan. This promise would become central to the Old Testament. Furthermore, each Hebrew family originally had ancestral land, the title to which they carefully guarded (as Naboth did in 1 Kings 21:3, "The LORD forbid that I should give you the inheritance of my fathers"). While, as a result of the Exile, virtually no one in Palestine was living on his or her original ancestral land, many not only in Palestine but also in Asia Minor did have land and other possessions that had been passed down for generations. An inheritance showed that you belonged somewhere, and it was also security for yourself and your offspring. Persecution affected one's inheritance, as hostile neighbors might drive one from ancestral land, possessions might be destroyed by mobs, or the government might confiscate both goods and land (as Jason risked in Acts 17:8–9). First Peter points to an inheritance that cannot be touched by human hostility, for it is stored in a place where human beings cannot reach.

Who through faith are shielded by God's power (1:5). The concept of being shielded by a great power was familiar in the ancient world. Having a powerful patron was one form of protection people sought. The Roman Empire as a whole was viewed as protecting its inhabitants from the chaotic and destructive peoples along the borders of the empire, such as the Parthians to the east. Likewise the Roman peace (*pax Romana*) prevented one province or city-state of the empire from attacking another. Various gods were also viewed as protecting their adherents. In the Old Testament God is often spoken of as a shield.[4] Christians, Peter asserts, do have a shielding power, not one which they can physically see, such as a patron or Roman legions, but (as in the Old Testament) God himself. Because they cannot see the power, faith is necessary.

Until the coming of the salvation that is ready to be revealed in the last time (1:5). Salvation was also a common idea in the ancient world. It could mean physical deliverance, political deliverance (such as that through Roman armies), or spiritual deliverance. For non-Christians the latter might be enlightenment achieved through a pagan cult or deliverance from some curse or problem, achieved through magic. For pagans deliverance, even when future, was normally thought of as within this lifetime or world. Christians could similarly speak of salvation (which for them was ultimately physical and political as well as spiritual)[5] in three tenses. At times, although rarely, they spoke of salvation in the past, "I was saved."[6] Somewhat more frequently they spoke of it in the present, "I am being saved."[7] Peter focuses on the most frequent tense, the future, "I will be saved," for the Christians to whom he was writing certainly did not feel delivered in their present circumstances.[8] (Nor might Peter, if he wrote this during imprisonment in Rome.) The full deliverance does already exist, but it will only be revealed "in the last time."

The idea of deliverance at the very end of this age was deeply embedded in Jewish and Christian literature, especially apocalyptic literature like Daniel and Revelation in the Bible and *1 Enoch* or some of the *Testaments of the Twelve Patriarchs* outside of the Bible. Likewise the Dead Sea Scrolls spoke of such an expectation. For instance, the War Scroll presents a final battle during which the deliverance of God appears as the faithful fight a final battle. Thus anyone who had read Jewish or Christian literature would have been familiar with this idea.

In this you greatly rejoice, though now for a little while you may have had to suffer grief in all kinds of trials (1:6). The contrast of present trials (or tests) and joy is common in New Testament literature, indicating that these were common teachings in the early church. James 1:2 uses exactly the same phrase for "all kinds of trials" ("trials of many kinds" in the NIV) and also contrasts this with joy. Likewise Romans 5:3 says, "We also rejoice in our sufferings," using different wording, but expressing the same idea. Ultimately such teaching went back to Jesus: "Blessed are you when people insult you, persecute you and falsely say all kinds of evil against you because of me. Rejoice and be glad, because great is your reward in heaven, for in the same way they persecuted the prophets who were before you" (Matt. 5:11–12).

"LIKE THE FLOWERS OF THE FIELD. . ."

A field of wildflowers near Capernaum.

The rejoicing is not because one enjoys persecution or because one denies the reality of pain and suffering (or because one ignores it, as in the *apatheia* of the Stoics); rather, it is because the Christian has an eschatological perspective. That is, he or she understands that at the end of the age God will pay back each person for the evil they have suffered as a result of their allegiance to him; therefore they can rejoice now, in anticipation of the coming heavenly reward.

The tests or trials (Gk. *peirasmos*) mentioned in any of these passages are not those that are the common lot of all humanity, and certainly not illness (which uses a different vocabulary),[9] but those that result from the person's commitment to Jesus. These might be the pains of direct persecution, or they might be the struggles of Christian service (e.g., Paul's list in 2 Cor. 11:23–29). Certainly this was the experience of the Christians to whom our letter is addressed.

Your faith—of greater worth than gold, which perishes even though refined by fire—may be proved genuine (1:7). The believers addressed in this letter are given the hope that their faith (or, better, commitment to Jesus) would be proved genuine, like genuine gold remains when put into a refiner's fire and other things that look like gold are burned up or removed as waste. (The same root in Greek is translated in the NIV "refined" and "proved genuine" here and "testing" in James 1:3.) Not only do James and 1 Peter use similar language and imagery, but so did earlier Jewish literature. *Wisdom of Solomon* 3:5–6 states, "Having been disciplined a little, [the righteous] will receive great good, because God tested them and found them worthy of himself; like gold in the furnace he tried them, and like a sacrificial burnt offering he accepted them" (NRSV). The Christian version of the saying, built on Jewish roots, was apparently popular with early Christian teachers, for 1 Peter, James, and Paul (Rom. 5:3–5) all use differing forms of it.

You are receiving the goal of your faith, the salvation of your souls (1:9). The author is not thinking here of soul as opposed to body, but "soul" in its meaning "life" or "self."[10] The goal of commitment to Jesus is that when he appears, the lives or selves of these believers will be delivered because they belong to him. Again salvation is viewed as future, for in the present they are not experiencing a lot of deliverance, but rather persecution and rejection.

The prophets, who spoke of the grace that was to come to you (1:10). In the ancient world something that was old and deeply rooted in tradition was valued more than something that was new and innovative. In pointing to the prophetic announcement of coming deliverance (we do not know what specific passages Peter has in mind, although the reference to "the sufferings of Christ and the glories that would follow" [1:11] suggests passages such as Ps. 22 and Isa. 53, or perhaps a combination of passages), Peter locates salvation as something old, traditional, and valuable.

The Spirit of Christ (1:11). The Spirit is so named to underline the fact that the Spirit who spoke about Christ had animated the prophets and the same "Holy Spirit sent from heaven" (1:12) had brought the gospel to them. Jews certainly believed that God's Spirit had animated the prophets (although they would not have called him "the Spirit of

Christ"); they were divided as to whether the Spirit departed after the time of Ezra (one part of the proto-rabbinic tradition asserts this) or whether there was a continuing prophetic tradition (most other Jewish traditions, including parts of the proto-rabbinic tradition).[11] Peter places the gospel within this tradition, tracing it back to the ancient prophets.

Even angels long to look into these things (1:12). Angelology was important in the Jewish world, and the names of angels are mentioned in books like *1 Enoch* and the Dead Sea Scroll *4Q Songs of the Sabbath Sacrifice*. The law was exalted because it was given through the mediation of angels (Heb. 2:2, following Jewish thought). Peter indicates that the suffering Christians are privileged above the ancient prophets and holy angels, a teaching also found in Hebrews 1:14 and 2:16.

These Christians have been told by their neighbors that they have abandoned their ancestral traditions, but in fact they stand in a most ancient tradition. They have probably been told that they have abandoned the gods, but in fact the angels above envy them and the Holy Spirit of God is the one who has brought the gospel to them and whom they have experienced at conversion. They are "plugged into" heaven. Throughout the whole thanksgiving Peter has countered their sense of alienation by emphasizing that they belong to heaven, have a reward coming, are related to God, and even stand in an ancient tradition.

The Call to Holiness (1:13–2:10)

Prepare your minds for action; be self-controlled (1:13). This expression depicts a person getting ready for active work by tucking up the skirt of a garment into a belt and tightening it so the legs would be free. "Self-controlled" is the opposite of intoxication; thus Peter means thinking soberly and clearly in the light of the coming revelation of Jesus.

Do not conform to the evil desires (1:14). This means living in contrast to their former pagan lifestyle that was characterized by following their desires (the word "evil" is not in the original text). For Greeks any life controlled by changing desires was less worthy than one directed by sober thought, while for the Jews the inclination towards evil (*yēṣer*) was nothing more than desire without the boundaries set by the law. Thus control by desire is characterized as "ignorance" of either rational thought (Greek, including the Jew Philo) or God's law (most Jews).

As obedient children (1:14). Peter has already implied his readers are God's children when he wrote about being born anew and having an inheritance. Now he suggests the commonplace idea in the Mediterranean world that they should obey and be like the character of the father of the family. This was part of upholding the honor of the family and its father, the opposite of shaming the family.[12]

"Be holy, because I am holy" (1:16). In Leviticus 19:2 this clause appears in the context of regulations related to topics of the Ten Commandments (Lev. 11:45 and 20:7 also contain it in different contexts). Peter is contrasting such moral holiness to a life controlled by desires and so is using it of moral purity, as Jesus did when he used a similar phrase in Matthew 5:48, "Be perfect, therefore, as your heavenly Father is perfect." Jesus, of course, was not referring to absolute perfection, but the type of perfection that Noah had (Gen. 6:9–"blameless" in the NIV translates the same word for "perfect" that is in Matthew). Noah, of course, was a human person who lived a life pleasing to God.

A Father who judges each [person's] work impartially (1:17). We may be God's children, but our "Father" is an impartial judge. Impartiality (as opposed to taking bribes or considering the social standing of the plaintiffs) was a key characteristic of a righteous judge in the Old Testament. Deuteronomy 16:18–20 instructs, "Appoint judges and officials for each of your tribes in every town the LORD your God is giving you, and they shall judge the people fairly. Do not pervert justice or show partiality. Do not accept a bribe, for a bribe blinds the eyes of the wise and twists the words of the righteous. Follow justice and justice alone, so that you may live and possess the land the LORD your God is giving you." As the supreme judge God is supremely impartial. He is indeed Father, but that does not mean that his children can get away with behavior he would condemn in others. This means that even though they are "away from home" (i.e., "strangers here" [1 Peter 1:17]) they should live with "respectful fear." While the term "respectful" is not in the Greek text, what is implied is the fear a child would have of a father if the child were considering some act the father would punish. The analogy was even clearer in that world than in ours, for fathers in that culture were more emotionally distant from the family and wielded more authority over the family.[13]

You were redeemed (1:18). While this verse is another indication that the readers were Gentile Christians, the focus is on the idea of redemption. The readers would have been familiar with the concept of purchasing themselves or an enslaved friend or relative out of slavery and the redeeming of prisoners of war by their friends or their country.[14]

The precious blood of Christ (1:19). While sacrifice is common in the Old Testament and was practiced in most Mediterranean cultures, here there is probably a specific reference to the Passover sacrifice, which could be a goat, but was often a lamb. Like most sacrifices, it had to be without "blemish or defect," although this pairing of the two words is New Testament, not Old Testament. Naturally Christ is greater than the Passover since that animal was chosen on the tenth of Nisan (the Jewish month falling in the March–April period) and sacrificed on the fourteenth, while Jesus was "chosen before the creation of the world" and "revealed" a few decades earlier than this letter ("revealed" probably includes the whole complex of events—Jesus' incarnation, life, death, and resurrection). Jesus is thus the greater Passover.

Obeying the truth (1:22) is Peter's concept of turning to Christ. It comes across clearly in the commands in Acts 2:38 ("Peter replied, 'Repent and be baptized, every one of you, in the name of Jesus Christ for the forgiveness of your sins. And you will receive the gift of the Holy Spirit'"); 2:40; and 17:30 ("He [God] commands all people everywhere to repent").

Born again . . . of imperishable [seed] (1:23). This image expands on the idea of "new birth" (1:3) with a reference to the sperm (i.e., seed) of our Father (an image used in John 1:12; James 1:18; and 1 John 3:9). This is identified as "the living and enduring word of God," that is, the gospel message.

All men are like grass . . . but the word of the Lord stands forever (1:24–25). This quotation in 1:24–25 is from the Greek version of Isaiah 40:6b–8, a text that in Isaiah refers to human frailty versus the certainty of God's promise of redemption, using images drawn from the hot desert wind's withering the vegetation in its path. Peter is not the only New Testament writer to use this passage (cf. James 1:10–11), and it fits well in this context. While their experience of life under persecution might be that "the grass withers and the flowers fall," it is really their pagan persecutors who "are like grass," while they have been born of "the word of the Lord [that] stands forever." In an insecure world they have security through the power of the gospel.

Rid yourselves of all malice and all deceit, hypocrisy, envy, and slander of every kind (2:1). The vices listed are similar to the various vice catalogues in the New Testament (e.g., James 3:14–16: "bitter envy and selfish ambition. . . . For where you have envy and selfish ambition, there you find disorder and every evil practice") that stress anger, envy, and similar sins that destroy Christian community, rather than murder and sexual sins that were presumed to be issues only in their pre-Christian past (1 Cor. 6:9–10 and Gal. 5:19–21 do include sexual sins, because at least in Corinth they were issues for the Christian community). Paul mentions slander in 2 Corinthians 12:20 ("quarreling, jealousy, outbursts of anger, factions, slander, gossip, arrogance and disorder") and in Ephesians 4:31 ("Get rid of all bitterness, rage and anger, brawling and slander, along with every form of malice"), whereas James goes on to reject

REFLECTIONS

IN THE WESTERN WORLD OUR tendency is to look on new birth as an individual affair and salvation as a past possession, rather than viewing new birth as something that places us in a new family with a new Father and new brothers and sisters and salvation as a future goal. Could that be why the vices Peter mentions, which destroy the Christian family, are readily tolerated among us rather than being rejected in favor of sincere love?

The Image of the Temple

The temple as a building appeared firm and unmovable in the New Testament Jewish world. Such a structure provided a picture of security to the persecuted Christians. It appealed to other Jewish groups as well. The Dead Sea Scroll 1QS 8:7 calls the council of the community a "precious cornerstone, whose foundations shall neither rock nor sway in their place," although the Targum on Isaiah 28 referred the cornerstone image to the king or the Messiah.

In our passage, a master mason, God, selects a stone, Jesus, that others have rejected (a reference to the crucifixion) and finds it just the stone for his building project. Jesus is the "cornerstone" (2:6) on which the building rests (thus the quotation is from Isa. 28:16, which Rom. 9:33 and Eph. 2:20 also use—this shows that the church as a whole, not just Peter, used these passages).

hypocrisy and anger by stressing the opposite virtue (James 3:17).

Like newborn babies, crave pure spiritual milk (2:2). The image of newborn babies fits with the references to "new birth" and divine "seed." Notice that "milk" does not mean the same here as it does in 1 Corinthians 3:2 and Hebrews 5:12–13. There it is a metaphor for the basics of the faith that Christians should grow beyond, while here it means spiritual teaching that one should never outgrow. This fact underlines the danger of defining a metaphorical term in one place by its use in another.

The living Stone (2:4). . . . You also, like living stones, are being built into a spiritual house (2:5) . . . a chosen and precious cornerstone (2:6). The image shifts from family to temple. Drawing on the phrase "Come to him" in the Greek version of Psalm 34:5, our author does not entirely leave the realm of people (the stones are living), but does shift the imagery to a temple (see "The Image of the Temple"). Jesus is as solid as the temple and thus security for those who trust in him, but he is a consternation and rock in the way for those who reject him (using Ps. 118:22, where "cornerstone" may be the better translation than "capstone," and Isa. 8:14). Chaining together of commonly used texts (called *testamonia*) is a typical style of Jewish exegesis.

Jesus as the cornerstone, however, is only one side of the imagery of the temple. The Christians are also chosen by God and built into the walls alongside Jesus. (Such imagery was also used by Jewish groups; for example, the Dead Sea Scroll 1QS 5:6 describes that community as "a house of holiness for Israel.") The process is ongoing, for the church is still being built as more and more people obey Christ.

Holy priesthood, offering spiritual sacrifices (2:5). The imagery shifts from the solid, unmovable walls of the temple to the Christians as the priesthood within the temple. Readers of the Old Testament, whether Jew or Gentile, would be aware of the Aaronic priesthood. Furthermore, all of them had seen pagan priests, even though none may have seen the priests in Jerusalem. The Christians are priests because, unlike a building, people do something. What they do is offer, not physical sacrifices of incense and animals as in the Old Testament, but

FOUNDATION STONES

The foundation of the temple of Apollo at Delphi.

REFLECTIONS

GOD DEFINES HIS PEOPLE BY THEIR center, Jesus, and their orientation, worship, not their boundaries (who is in and who is out). What does this say about how we define our church? Would such a focus strengthen our worship life? Might it now be important for us individually as well?

spiritual sacrifices. (Peter does not specify what they are; the analogy of Hebrews 13:15–16 suggests that he is thinking of praise and charitable deeds)

A chosen people, a royal priesthood, a holy nation, a people belonging to God (2:9). This image is more specific than a general reference to Old Testament priesthood. Any of the readers familiar with the Old Testament would recognize the weaving together of Exodus 19:5–6 and Isaiah 43:20–21: ". . . out of all nations you will be my treasured possession. Although the whole earth is mine, you will be for me a kingdom of priests and a holy nation" and, "I provide water in the desert and streams in the wasteland, to give drink to my people, my chosen, the people I formed for myself that they may proclaim my praise." As other New Testament writers also do, Peter is calling these Gentile Christians by the titles God gave to Israel in the desert.[15] For him there are not two covenants, one for the Jews and another for Gentile Christians, but one covenant, which the Gentiles, who once "were not a people," have been brought into and made "the people of God" (1 Peter 2:10), while

Household Duties

The phrase "Household Duties" or *Haustafel* (German for "Table of Household Duties") is used to refer to the descriptions of duties or household codes in the letters of Paul and in 1 Peter.[A-1] The bulk of this ethical teaching has to do with relationships within the household: husband–wife; father–children; master–slave. First Peter also includes a section on the relationship of the household to the state, whereas Paul discusses a similar topic in Romans 13 outside of the household duty structure.

The reason the authors include this material is that Christianity was viewed as subversive to the household and therefore to the good order of the city or state. That is, inviting wives, slaves, and children to believe in Christ whether or not the *pater familias* (male head of the household) did was clearly a rejection of his traditional authority to determine the religion of the whole household. These codes, then, make it clear that the traditional cultural submission of wives, slaves, and children is still valid, although it is now "in Christ" (as part of their overriding commitment to him and so limited by what he would approve of).

The codes also had another function insofar as Paul and Peter (1 Peter 3:7) described the ways the male household head should serve his wife, children, and slaves. This was not part of the traditional cultural teaching; it might even shock the male readers to hear that they had a responsibility to serve those whom they had learned should serve them. To hear that their wives were equal heirs of God's grace (3:7) or that they should behave towards them like Christ's giving his life for the good of the church (rather than as Christ ruling in heaven, Eph. 5:25) would have been a novel idea for most converts, one that turned their ideas of what was right order on its head. This, of course, is like what Jesus did to the idea of how a Messiah should behave. Paul and Peter are applying the teaching of Jesus to the household, not as a revolution from below but as a revolution from above. The one with power gives up power in the service of others, just as Jesus did.

So the *Haustafeln* had two roles. First, they reassured the Greco-Roman world that the church was not subversive of good order as defined by the culture. That is, they taught the women, slaves, and children to live out submission without compromising their allegiance to Christ. Second, they taught male heads of families to follow the example of Christ and lay aside their privileges for the good of those who were their underprivileged equals.[A-2] those Jews and others who do not believe in Jesus stumble and fall from their natural heritage in the covenant.

How to Relate to Society so as to Minimize Persecution (2:11–4:11)

In the previous section Peter has clearly explained the Christians' identity. However, the non-Christian society around them remains a reality they must deal with. This next section, often referred to as an example of a Table of Household Duties, advises them on how to do this so as to minimize conflict.

Aliens and strangers (2:11). This phrase indicated their low status in this world. Foreigners were those who lacked the rights and privileges of citizens. Thus they were only a step above slaves, who lacked freedom and personhood. Yet in practice slaves of socially important masters would have received more respect than a foreigner.

Abstain from sinful desires (2:11). While many Greek philosophers, especially the Stoics, also saw "sinful (Greek "fleshly") desires" as the enemy of true virtue, in their view the body and its emotions and desires were evil *per se*. Peter follows the more Jewish view that human desires will lead one astray if they are not controlled by a higher principle, which for the Jew was the law. The strategy advised is that by controlling desire the pagans would see the Christians leading the lives of virtue that philosophers talked about, but that the people as a whole lacked the power to accomplish.

On the day he visits us (2:12). This clause means when God comes to judge (using the Old Testament image of God "visiting" in judgment and salvation, e.g., Jer. 15:15, "You understand, O LORD; remember me and care for me. Avenge me on my persecutors"). The pagans will have to admit then that God had been honored by his people's virtue.

The king, as the supreme authority (2:13). The first example of the "good deeds" mentioned in 2:12 is that of submitting to the ruling Caesar, or king, and his representatives. Whereas pagan authors often called for absolute obedience to the ruler, Peter conditions this submission by pointing out that it is "for the Lord's sake" and that the ruler is a humanly created authority ("authority instituted among men"), not a divine authority. Rulers often claimed divine appointment and even divine status (for most Roman emperors this was granted after death, although in some provinces the citizens began rites of worship while the emperor still lived).[16] Peter rejects this absolute right and points to an authority above the ruler for whose sake submission is given (and thus submission could not include anything which the Lord would not want) and the human origin of the government.

To punish those who do wrong and to commend those who do right (2:14).

right ▶

NERO

The image of the emperor (A.D. 54–68) appears on this coin.

The Roman governor was sent to a province to promote the order of Rome in that place. They usually spent the first part of their day hearing cases in order to punish evildoers (Mark 15:1, 25, are accurate pointers to the practice of dealing with such business early in the day). Peter asserts that this ideal of government is good. Yet everyone in the empire

◀ *left*

"FREEDOM"

A *libertas* coin celebrating freedom in the Roman empire.

knew that such justice was the ideal, not the reality of Roman emperors and governors. The emperor at the end of Peter's life was Nero, who, while starting off well enough, was the first emperor to persecute Christians. The governors were the Roman proconsuls (Senatorial provinces) or procurators (imperial provinces) appointed by Rome, whom even some Romans (e.g. the emperor Tiberius) realized enriched themselves through graft.[17] However, whether or not the person's character deserved it, showing proper respect would "silence the ignorant talk of foolish" people, for some non-believers looked on the Christian movement as a seditious movement that was undermining the good order of the empire.

Slaves, submit yourselves to your masters with all respect (2:18). The slaves, the second example Peter gives, was not viewed as a moral person, but rather as one who was simply to obey unquestioningly. Thus even in addressing them Peter is raising their status. The slaves had few rights and could be treated by their masters arbitrarily. Thus the dichotomy of "good and considerate" and "those who are harsh" was a known part of life. While some slaves were treated well and were educated at the master's expense, a slave could also be abused or beaten for little or no reason. Thus it was quite possible that a slave would "suffer for doing good." Furthermore, the slave, unlike the Roman citizen, could be crucified. Thus Peter urges them to identify with Jesus, who also suffered the extreme penalty, which was so shameful that Roman writers would rarely mention it.[18]

"He committed no sin, and no deceit was found in his mouth" (2:22). The example of Christ is cited from Isaiah 53:9. Peter alludes to this passage in Isaiah several more times: he "bore our sins in his body on the tree" (2:24) = Isaiah 53:5, 12; "he made no threats" (2:23) = Isaiah 53:7; "you were like sheep going astray" (2:25) = Isaiah 53:6. It is identification with Jesus that gives dignity to their suffering.

Shepherd and Overseer (2:25). This image of Christ comes from Ezekiel 34:11–16, which begins, "For this is what the Sovereign LORD says: I myself will search for my sheep and look after them." Peter will pick up the image again in 5:1–4, applying it to church leadership.

Wives, in the same way be submissive to your husbands (3:1). Peter's third example of doing good is addressed to the wives of non-Christian husbands (the whole focus of the passage is evangelistic). Wives in most of the Roman Empire were expected to adhere to the religion of their husbands. Christianity was viewed as subversive in that it invited women to commit themselves to Jesus whether or not their husbands approved. By being generally "submissive to [their] husbands" they would be living up to pagan virtue, although their submission was not to extend to disobedience to Christ, such as doing immoral acts or worshiping pagan gods (how would that show either "purity" or "reverence"?). Our author expected that such exemplary behavior would mean that the husbands would "be won over without words by the behavior of their wives." Since husbands were often significantly older than their wives (the Roman ideal was a man of thirty marrying a woman of fifteen), as well as better educated, this nonverbal approach to evangelism was appropriate.

Not . . . from outward adornment, such as braided hair and the wearing of gold jewelry and fine clothes (3:3). Since men often displayed their wealth and social status in the dress of their wives, some "outward adornment" might be the wishes of a husband and thus an expression of submission. Yet both Jewish and pagan writers often advised men to prohibit their wives from dressing up.[19] The Jewish *Testament of Reuben* 5:5 states: ". . .order your wives and your daughters not to adorn their heads and their appearances so as to deceive men's sound minds." With this sentiment the Stoics Seneca and Epictetus agreed.[20] Epictetus said:

> Immediately after they are fourteen [i.e., at puberty, when they were eligible for marriage], women are called "ladies" by men. So when they see that they have nothing else but only to be the bedfellows of men, they begin to beautify themselves, and put all their hopes in that. It is worth while for us to take pains, therefore, to make them understand that they are honored for nothing else but only for appearing modest and self-respecting.[21]

This same idea was probably a frequent teaching in the churches, as 1 Timothy 2:9 uses almost identical language. What is clear is that such teaching applied only to upper-class women, whose husbands sometimes approved of their attending synagogue or church as a possible morally uplifting, harmless indulgence in a foreign superstition. Lower-class women and slaves often had only a single set of clothing and no jewelry at all. Note that the form of this statement is wisdom teaching, not law. Peter is not saying that women should never wear jewelry, but that virtue rather than adornment should be their focus.

A gentle and quiet spirit (3:4). "Gentle" means an amiable friendliness in contrast to roughness, bad temper, or brusqueness. These virtues were also valued in women by pagan writers.[22] "Quiet" (also appearing in the NT in 1 Tim. 2:2) is the opposite of restless, rebellious, or insubordinate. Thus up to this point Peter has not said

right ▶

BRAIDED HAIR

Julia Domina, the second wife of the emperor Severus (A.D. 193–211).

anything that a pagan moralist might not have said. He is advising women to live up to the best common morality of their day. It is only when he mentions the worth of this virtue "in God's sight" and goes on to refer to "the holy women of the past," meaning Hebrew and Jewish heroines of the faith, that Peter gives a motivation that goes beyond the best of pagan ethics. Christians live up to the best of their culture, but for better reasons.

Sarah, who obeyed Abraham and called him her master (3:6). This refers to Genesis 18:12, "After I am worn out and my master is old, will I now have this pleasure?" The Hebrew word for "master" (*'adonai*) can mean that, but it is also a typical Hebrew word for husband ("husband" is probably the better translation in Genesis). In the Greek version of the Old Testament, *'adonai* was translated by *kyrios*, a word meaning "sir," "master," or "lord," which allows Peter to make his point that Sarah thought of her husband respectfully (even if in Genesis she is laughing at God's promise when she does so).

Do not give way to fear (3:6). The allusion is to Proverbs 3:25–26 ("Have no fear of sudden disaster or of the ruin that overtakes the wicked, for the LORD will be your confidence and will keep your foot from being snared"), which uses two of the same Greek words as 1 Peter 3:6. Husbands then as now might try to intimidate their wives into giving up the faith or otherwise disobeying Jesus. The same Lord for whose sake they were generally submissive is the Lord, whom no threat or intimidation could keep them from obeying.

Be considerate as you live with your wives, and treat them with respect as the weaker partner and as heirs with you of the gracious gift of life (3:7). When he turns briefly to husbands, Peter makes the assumption that their wives are Christians ("heirs with you of the gracious gift of life"), for normally a pagan wife would follow her husband into his new belief. Rather than use his socially sanctioned power, the husband is to "be considerate" (lit., "live knowledgeably") and "treat [her] with respect," which is normally what one did to a person to whom one owed respect and deference. Here "considerate" means to recognize the one who is "weaker" (following both Jewish and pagan observations that women were physically weaker than men and thus vulnerable).[23] Notice that the New Testament never follows the pagan idea that women were weaker in mind or morally inferior to men. One treats her with respect by recognizing her as an equal in every way (lit., "fellow heir with you").

So that nothing will hinder your prayers (3:7). This clause may refer to the Old Testament teaching that God is the protector of the weak.[24] Peter implies that because of this God will not hear the prayers of one who is taking advantage of the vulnerability of his wife.

REFLECTIONS

IN HIS INSTRUCTIONS FOR THE CHRISTIAN HOUSEHOLD, Peter demonstrates a willingness to fit the cultural values of his day (e.g., those of marriage and slavery) insofar as they do not violate allegiance to Christ. Do we have the same willingness today, neither clinging onto values that society used to hold but no longer does, nor separating from society over values that are part of our Christian subculture rather than truly a matter of allegiance to Christ? Would this make it clear to our society what being a Christian really means and thus assist the witness of the church?

Live in harmony with one another; be sympathetic, love as brothers, be compassionate and humble (3:8). The summary list of virtues in 3:8 binds the community together, as a similar list bound the people of the Dead Sea Scrolls together: "a spirit of humility, patience, abundant charity, unending goodness . . . great charity towards all the sons of truth" (1QS 4:3ff.). Thus there are Jewish precedents for these virtues.

Do not repay evil with evil or insult with insult, but with blessing, because to this you were called so that you may inherit a blessing (3:9). This teaching of nonretaliation because one is aware of God's coming reward recalls Jesus' teaching: "Blessed are those who are persecuted because of righteousness, for theirs is the kingdom of heaven" (Matt. 5:10). This is amplified in 5:11 (which adds the idea of insult) and then even more in 5:38–48. Peter follows up the allusion to Jesus by quoting Psalm 34:13–17 in the next three verses. He has already cited Psalm 34:8 in 1 Peter 2:3 (Heb. 6:5 cites it as well), so this psalm was clearly a favorite in the early church. The psalmist is concerned with long life on earth, but in Peter's context it refers to the eternal life and heavenly inheritance he mentioned in chapter 1.

But even if you should suffer for what is right, you are blessed (3:14). This too is an allusion to the teaching of Jesus in Matthew 5:10 (see above), for suffering vocabulary usually refers to persecution and "for what is right" is equivalent to "righteousness."

"Do not fear what they fear; do not be frightened" (3:14). Peter cites the Greek version of Isaiah 8:12–13. In the Old Testament this refers to the fear of the Aram-Israel alliance (Kings Rezin and Pekah), who planned to remove Ahaz from the throne of Judah in order to place someone there who would join them in their alliance against Assyria. In 1 Peter the statement refers to fear of persecutors.

In your hearts set apart Christ as Lord (3:15). This instruction also comes from Isaiah 8:13, "The LORD Almighty is the one you are to regard as holy, he is the one you are to fear, he is the one you are to dread." The quotation is shifted from God to Christ by changing two words found in the Greek version of Isaiah.[25] In the Isaiah context it is part of a promise of salvation, and this is implicit in 1 Peter as well. Rather than fear people, Christians are to answer them confidently, although also "with gentleness" (a virtue of wives in 3:4 above, now to be part of every Christian life) "and respect," a point sometimes forgotten by modern apologists.

Be prepared to give an answer (3:15). This instruction likely depends on the teaching of Jesus in places like Luke 12:4–12, but Jews also taught similarly: R. Eleazar said, "Be alert to study the Law and know how to make an answer to the unbeliever" (*m. ᵓAbot* 2:14).

Those who speak maliciously against your good behavior in Christ may be ashamed of their slander (3:16). The shame refers to shame at final judgment. Christians were slandered as "haters of humankind" (because they would not go to pagan festivals and parties), traitors to the state (because they called Christ and not Caesar Lord and also because they refused to worship the genius of the emperor), and immoral (because in pagan eyes their warm love for their "brothers and sisters" was thought to be sexual and it was even rumored that they ate flesh and drank blood at their meals, which was thought to have come from infants they had slaughtered).[26]

Later (A.D.177) Athenagoras states in his *Legatio pro Christianis* 3, "Three things are alleged against us: atheism, Thyestean feasts, Oedipodian intercourse." Atheism came from their not worshiping the various Greco-Roman deities; Thyestean feasts showed a belief that they ate real human flesh and drank human blood; and Oedipodian intercourse indicated the belief that they had sexual intercourse with their "brothers and sisters."

Christ died for sins . . . the righteous for the unrighteous (3:18). The idea that something dies for sins is common in the Old Testament in sacrificial contexts, e.g., Leviticus 5:7, "If he cannot afford a lamb, he is to bring two doves or two young pigeons to the LORD as a penalty for his sin—one for a sin offering and the other for a burnt offering" (the "as a penalty for his sin" is the same in the Greek version of the Old Testament as "for sins" in 1 Peter 3:18). In saying "the righteous for the unrighteous" Peter again reminds his readers of Isaiah 53, this time 53:11: "After the suffering of his soul, he will see the light of life and be satisfied; by his knowledge my righteous servant will justify many, and he will bear their iniquities." Peter's point, of course, is not simply that his readers identify with Jesus' suffering, but that they see that he went through suffering to exaltation.

The Spirits and Genesis 6

Who are the "spirits in prison" in 1 Peter 3:19? Some argue that these are human spirits from the people who died in Noah's day. However, in the New Testament "spirit" by itself never refers to a human spirit. When a human being is referred to, the word is always qualified, such as a "man's spirit" in 1 Corinthians 2:11. Normally humans existing apart from the body are called "souls" (as in Rev. 6:9). Therefore it is probable that this passage refers to nonhuman spiritual beings.

According to the text, these spirits existed and "disobeyed . . . in the days of Noah." Elsewhere the Bible refers three times to beings who fit this description: Genesis 6:1–2; 2 Peter 2:4–5; Jude 6. The two New Testament passages refer to Genesis 6, "When men began to increase in number on the earth and daughters were born to them, the sons of God saw that the daughters of men were beautiful, and they married any of them they chose." While the Old Testament does not refer to the fate of these beings, both 2 Peter and Jewish tradition do. For example, *1 Enoch* describes the fall of the angels in chapter 6 and their imprisonment in chapter 10. Then Enoch intercedes for them in chapters 12–13, which intercession is rejected. Then in chapter 21 he says, "And I came to an empty place. And I saw there neither a heaven above nor an earth below, but a chaotic and terrible place. And there I saw seven stars of heaven [angels are called stars, angels, spirits or Watchers in *1 Enoch*] bound together in it . . . I said, 'For what sin are they bound . . . ?' Then one of the holy angels . . . spoke to me and said to me . . . 'These are among the stars of heaven which have transgressed the commandments of the Lord and are bound in this place until the completion of ten million years. . . .'" Enoch goes on and sees a worse place and is told, "'This place is the prison house of the angels; they are detained here forever.'" The location of the prison is not always specified in Jewish tradition, but some traditions locate it in the second heaven,[A-3] which would be appropriate for 1 Peter if Jesus' ascension is in view.

Was put to death in the body but made alive by the Spirit (3:18). This is not the best translation. Better would be: "He was put to death from the point of view of the physical world, but made alive from the point of view of the spiritual world." That is, 1 Peter is making a distinction between the present state and the resurrection state, similar to what Paul makes in 1 Corinthians 15:35–57.

Went and preached to the spirits in prison (3:19). It was "in this resurrection state" (a better translation than "through whom") that Jesus "went and preached to the spirits in prison." As to the identity of these spirits, see "The Spirits and Genesis 6." Wherever this prison is located, Peter is referring to Jesus' resurrection proclamation of triumph, vindicating the justice of God and sealing the fate of the fallen angels as he ascends into heaven.

God waited patiently in the days of Noah while the ark was being built. . . . In it only a few people, eight in all, were saved (3:20). This refers to Genesis 5:32; 7:6, which are often interpreted as indicating that the ark took a hundred years to build, and to 6:18; 7:7; 8:15, which all refer to Noah, his wife, his three sons, and their wives. The ark itself was a rectangular box 450 x 75 x 45 feet, containing three decks. There was ventilation at the top under the roof.

This water symbolizes baptism that now saves you also (3:21). The salvation in the ark is compared to baptism as practiced in Peter's day. In baptism the person officially pledged his or her commitment to Christ and therefore was only considered a Christian afterward. It was the official moment of salvation, much as we today consider persons married only after they have publicly pledged their commitment to one another, no matter how much they have pledged their commitment privately. Peter makes it clear that it is the sincere pledge, "the pledge of a good conscience," that saves, not simply the action of the water on the body. Furthermore, the power is found in "the resurrection of Jesus Christ."

He who has suffered in his body is done with sin (4:1). The principle itself is clear in Jesus' life, which forms the background for this whole passage. Once Jesus died, all of his dealings with sin were over. He could no longer be touched by it. It is also true for the Christian, for the choice of the path of suffering for Christ is at the same time a choice against sin.

He does not live the rest of his earthly life for evil human desires, but rather for the will of God (4:2). The word "evil" is not part of the Greek text. It may be implied, or Peter may be noting that even legitimate human desires are no longer primary motivations if one is choosing suffering in the will of God over against possible physical comfort by compromising the faith.

Debauchery, lust, drunkenness, orgies, carousing and detestable idolatry (4:3). Again 1 Peter refers to the fact that his addressees are pagan converts, not Jewish Christians, when he refers to their former life: Jews were known for neither orgies nor idolatry. This list is a stylized list of Jewish and Christian critique of paganism rather than giving specific examples of what these Christians had done in their pagan life. We see this in that (1) many pagan philosophers also condemned these same vices (except idolatry, which was approved, at least when it showed allegiance to family and the state), (2) Jews had long made similar condemnations of pagans and paganizing Jews (e.g., *Testament of Moses* 7:3–10), and (3) only wealthier citizens could indulge in some of these things—the poor lived hand-to-mouth without extra income. Still, popular culture did not condemn such things.

They think it strange that you do not plunge with them into the same flood of dissipation (4:4). The Christian did not show up at the trade guild banquet in the temple of the patron deity, did not celebrate a family festival (also often in a pagan temple), did not celebrate national festivals, and did not attend some parties. Such behavior was considered so "unnatural" that the Christians must be against their family, trade, or city, devoid of human feelings and enjoyment, even a "hater of humanity."

Him who is ready to judge the living and the dead (4:5). This is a Jewish designation of God, as the rabbinic citation in *m. ʾAbot* 4:22 shows, "It is [God] that shall judge. . . . You shall hereafter give account and reckoning before the King of Kings, the Holy One, blessed be he."

The gospel was preached even to those who are now dead (4:6). These dead are not the imprisoned spirits of 3:19, but rather Christians who have died. As Christ was judged, human beings judge them in the physical world (a better translation than "in regard to the body"). They judge them either by killing them, as they did Christ, or by condemning their lifestyle and concluding at their death that their Christianity did not keep them from the common lot of humanity. Since there is little evidence of martyrdom in 1 Peter, such mockery is more likely what he is talking about, although actual martyrdom was not far off. Yet human beings do not have the last word: God does. As Jesus was resurrected "from the point of view of the spiritual world" (cf. 3:18), so they will "live according to God" in this spiritual world. The final verdict is God's resurrection.

The end of all things is near (4:7). While most Christians of the first generation expected the return of Christ and the end of the age within their lifetime, the clause itself refers to the idea that Jesus inaugurated the last stage of human history. Therefore the next major event on God's timetable was the final end of the age.

Clear minded and self-controlled (4:7). These were virtues that pagans as well as Christians admired. As in Romans 12:3 ("think of yourself with sober judgment, in accordance with the measure of faith God has given you"), this means a proper view of self and an avoidance of intoxication. A good, clear mind is presented as the best foundation for prayer.

DISSIPATION

This *amphoriskos* depicts a Roman orgiastic party.

Love covers over a multitude of sins (4:8). Proper relationships ("Love each other deeply") within the Christian community were important to Peter. Here he cites Proverbs 10:12, which was proverbial in the early church. By love our author is thinking of forgiving one another. He is not concerned about emotional feelings about other Christians, but rather concrete acts of kindness.

Offer hospitality (4:9). Hospitality meant offering food and lodging to traveling Christians. This was an important Jewish virtue centuries before Jesus.[27] In fact, later Jews would point to Abraham's receiving the travelers in Genesis 18:2–5 as evidence of his virtue,[28] and Job protests his virtue by saying, "The stranger has not lodged in the street; I have opened my doors to the traveler" (Job 31:32 NRSV). While there were some practical aspects to this (what inns there were in the Roman world were often associated with immoral behavior), the main idea was that a traveler was away from his or her family and clan and thus vulnerable. Offering food and housing was both an act of charity and an offer of protection in the home of one who belonged in the city.

Gift he [or she] **has received . . . God's grace in its various forms (4:10).** The early church believed the coming of the Spirit was the mark of the new age. One way one recognized the presence of the Spirit was by his or her gifts. All descriptions of spiritual gifts are *ad hoc* lists, examples given to fit the purpose of the author. So while Paul in 1 Corinthians 12 lists teaching, prophecy, and tongues as verbal gifts and only mentions administration, miracles, and healing as serving gifts, in Romans 12 encouraging appears as a verbal gift, and serving, contributing, and showing mercy appear in the serving category. Peter never tells us in this letter which gifts he might stress, for he gives only two categories, the one who "speaks" and the one who "serves." In this he divides gifts as Luke says that Peter did in Acts 6:2, where "word of God" is contrasted with "wait[ing] on tables."[29]

To him be the glory and the power for ever and ever. Amen (4:11). Doxologies punctuate 1 Peter (the other one is in 5:11) and occur throughout the New Testament as the closings to sections of letters.[30] They are, of course, also common in Revelation.

How to Live in a Context of Persecution (4:12–5:11)

Dear friends (4:12). This word (*agapētoi*, "beloved") is an indication that a new section of the letter, the closing of the body, is beginning. It is more a formal statement than an expression of a special relationship.

Painful trial (4:12). A more literal translation would be "fiery trial." Some believe that this refers to the burning of some Christians in Rome under Nero:

> Accordingly, an arrest was first made of all who confessed; then, upon their information, an immense multitude was convicted, not so much of the crime of arson [since Nero claimed the Christians were responsible for the great fire in Rome], as of hatred of the human race. Mockery of every sort was added to their deaths. Covered with the skins of beasts, they were torn by dogs and perished, or were nailed to crosses, or were doomed to the flames. These served to illuminate the night

when daylight failed. Nero had thrown open his gardens for the spectacle, and was exhibiting a show in the circus, while he mingled with the people in the dress of a charioteer or drove about in a chariot.[31]

There is no evidence that this persecution extended to the provinces where the recipients of this letter lived. It appears to have been confined to Rome. Moreover, 1 Peter never refers to the death of Christians, but to their suffering.

Persecution in the Early Church Period

In the first decades of the church's existence it quickly became clear that the church differed from the surrounding culture and that the culture did not like it, whether this culture was Jewish or Greco-Roman. This displeasure was expressed in a number of ways: (1) commands and threats (Acts 4:17, 21); (2) physical punishment (5:40); (3) fines and confiscation of goods (17:9; Heb. 10:34); (4) imprisonment (Acts 16:23–24); (5) mob violence and lynching (7:57–58); and (6) judicial execution (12:1–4). Along with these came public shaming and insults (Heb. 10:33; 1 Peter 4:4) and economic discrimination (part of the background of James). Christians did not fit in, and the surrounding culture was prepared to use all of the means at its disposal to force them to return to cultural conformity. While execution, particularly judicial execution, was apparently rare (e.g., Rev. 2:13 names only one martyr and 2:10 mentions prison, not execution) and often localized when it happened (e.g., Nero did execute Christians in the 64–68 period, but we only hear of executions in Rome), the other forms of persecution were certainly painful and at times even worse than execution (e.g., economic discrimination and confiscation of goods and property could lead to slow starvation if other members of the church did not share with those experiencing the loss). Execution became more common in the second and third centuries, but still remained sporadic and localized, affecting relatively small numbers of Christians.

What did the church do to "deserve" such treatment? (1) They refused to take part in the normal worship life of the household, city, or state. To their fellow citizens this implied a lack of loyalty and a rebellious spirit, an undermining of good order. (2) They refused to take part in family celebrations, guild feats, and other social events, because of the connection of such events to idolatry or immoral behavior. This led to stigmatizing the Christians as antisocial, "haters of humanity," and the like. (3) There was the Christian critique of their culture: the claim that the Messiah had come and been executed by the Jewish leaders (in the Jewish world) or the claim that the lifestyle of the people was immoral and/or that idols were meaningless (in the Greco-Roman world). (4) There were specific Christian practices (their acceptance of Gentiles, their "stealing" the Gentile "God-fearers," their gathering together in "secret" societies, their treating one another as brother and sister across class, gender, and racial lines). (5) There were false rumors about the Christians (they encouraged Jews not to circumcise their children; they ate the flesh and drank the blood of babies at their ritual meals; they held orgies behind closed doors, calling them "love feasts"; they caused riots everywhere they went). (6) They claimed that Jesus was Lord, while Caesar claimed to be the only Lord. Add to these six elements normal human suspicion, fear of loss of power in the face of a growing movement, and general jealousy, and one gets a ripe climate for all types of persecution.

Christians responded to this treatment with patient endurance, with explanations (both informal and in court situations) of their real beliefs and practices, with flight to other cities, and with communal support for those who were suffering. In doing this they modeled their response on the teaching of Jesus (e.g., "flee to the next city") and the example of Jesus.[A-4]

Therefore he is referring to the sharp persecution that the whole community is experiencing—fierce and painful as fire, but not literally fire.

Something strange were happening (4:12). It is not as if God had lost control or persecution was not supposed to happen to Christians. They agreed with Jewish writers that it is to be expected. Jesus ben Sira taught, for example, "My child, when you come to serve the Lord, prepare yourself for testing. Set your heart right and be steadfast, and do not be impetuous in time of calamity. . . . For gold is tested in the fire, and those found acceptable [to God] in the furnace of humiliation" (Sir. 2:1–5).

Participate in the sufferings of Christ (4:13). This imitation of Christ is frequently cited in the New Testament, whether in terms of personal example (Col. 1:24) or an example to follow (Phil. 2:5–11). It builds on Jesus' frequent command to "follow me." In a Jewish context to follow a rabbi meant not just to travel with him, but also learn his teaching and copy his lifestyle. In fact, the rabbi's lifestyle was an important part of the teaching (*halakah*, which refers to how one lives). It is not a surprise, then, that Paul and Peter would be so insistent that our lives should be patterned on that of Jesus.

Rejoice (4:13). See the comments on 1:6 (cf. James 1:2). One rejoices, not because one enjoys persecution, but because being joined to Christ in persecution is a sign of being joined to him "when his glory is revealed," that is, in his second coming. This is based on Jesus' teaching, such as Luke 6:22–23: "Blessed are you when men hate you, when they exclude you and insult you and reject your name as evil, because of the Son of Man. Rejoice in that day and leap for joy, because great is your reward in heaven. For that is how their fathers treated the prophets."

If you are insulted because of the name of Christ (4:14). Christians were originally called followers of "the Way" or disciples of Jesus of Nazareth. It was only in Antioch that they were called Christians (Acts 11:26)—which is the Jewish term *Messiah* ("anointed one") translated in Greek as "Christ." However, since this term was not a title for Greek-speakers as "Messiah" was for many Jews, it was taken as a proper name and followers of Christ were called Christians, those belonging to Christ. It was therefore under this name that they were persecuted.

The Spirit of glory and of God (4:14). Jesus promised that the Holy Spirit would rest on them, his followers, when they were persecuted: "Whenever you are arrested and brought to trial, do not worry beforehand about what to say. Just say whatever is given you at the time, for it is not you speaking, but the Holy Spirit" (Mark 13:11), or "the Holy Spirit will teach you at that time what you should say" (Luke 12:12). Acts reports that Stephen was full of the Spirit (Acts 6:15; 7:55), so the presence of the Spirit might lead to execution, not deliverance. Peter refers to the "Spirit of glory" in that (1) this contrasts with the insults they are receiving, and (2) it (along with "of God") points to the future that they will experience (cf. 1 Peter 1:7; 5:4; cf. Col. 3:4).

A meddler (4:15). This is a person who sticks her or her nose into other people's affairs (which would include an overzealous witness). The word appears here for the first time in Greek. It is later writers that make its meaning clear.

Suffer as a Christian (4:16). The quotation cited on 4:11 indicated that Christians were accused as criminals, but that the real basis for the accusation was their Christian commitment. Thus Peter is talking about the real basis of the charges, not the actual charge against them.

Do not be ashamed, but praise God that your bear that name (4:16). In that culture any public accusation and punishment

Honor/Shame and Its Meaning

In the world of which the New Testament is a part, honor and shame were the chief motivating values. Honor is a publicly acknowledged claim to value or worth; shame is the diminishing of such public worth. A person would be born into a family with a given level of honor according to the social status of the family and the behavior of the individuals in the family. The child would end up either maintaining that honor against challenges through acts of courage, generosity, or wisdom, or would diminish his own honor and that of his family through cowardice, lack of generosity, foolishness, and the like. For instance, when Paul speaks of his escape from Damascus, he speaks of it in terms of shame or weakness, for he did not display courage or valor, for example, by fighting to the death in the gate of Damascus (2 Cor. 11:30–33). As a Christian, however, Paul had a different value system. His non-Christian social values included racial purity and religious achievement (2 Cor. 11:22; Phil. 3:5–6), as well as courage and strength when suffering (2 Cor. 11:23–29). However, he put such values ("boasting") aside and instead pointed to shameful things ("weakness") as his badge of "honor" (2 Cor. 12:5, 9), for in that Christ's power and Christ's relationship to him were demonstrated (Phil. 3:7–11). In other words, his new sense of honor was drawn from relationship with Christ, who had been shamed in this world but honored by God.

This sense of honor and shame is not only in Paul, but is also apparent in Hebrews, 1 Peter, and elsewhere in the New Testament. In Hebrews, even though Christ was shamed by human beings (Heb. 12:2) he has superior honor to the various aspects of Judaism. Thus by identifying with Jesus, the readers will (1) be associated with the superior honor of Christ and (2) honor the God who so honored Christ (rather than insult or shame God and receive the consequences).

In 1 Peter the readers are being shamed by their neighbors (words like "abuse," "insult," and "slander" are used), but it is these neighbors who will receive shame at the final judgment (1 Peter 3:16). The readers' faith, however, will bring them honor when Christ returns (1:7), not shame (2:6). It is they who have the honorable titles given them by God (2:9).

In both Hebrews and 1 Peter, then, there is an attempt to reverse honor-shame valuations given by the outside culture. In Hebrews Christ is not less honorable than Judaism (which is what a return to Judaism would imply), but more honorable. In 1 Peter the believers are not shameful (as their fellow citizens claim), but honorable, and it is those "honorable" (in the eyes of this world) fellow citizens who are heading toward shame when Christ appears.

Thus, while North American society appears guilt motivated (internal feelings predominate), the society of the early church period was honor–shame motivated (external valuations were most important). The surrounding society used shame as a major weapon of persecution (and especially in the cross, where the shaming was as significant as the execution), and the New Testament writers argued for a reversal of values, showing that Christ and the Christians were in fact the more honorable.[A-5] would bring shame, so it is significant that Peter reframes the situation and tells the believer to feel proud ("praise God") rather than experience shame.

For it is time for judgment to begin with the family of God (4:17). The suffering the believers are experiencing is a type of purifying fire, a judgment. That God judges his children was well known to Jews: "For the Lord first judges Israel for the wrong she has committed and then he shall do the same for all the nations" (*T. Benj.* 100:8–9). The form of argument used here, "if this is so, how much more will that be so," was frequently used by Jewish writers. It was called *qal wahomer* or "light and heavy," as early as the time of Jesus (i.e., it is one of the seven hermeneutical rules of Hillel).

If it is hard for the righteous to be saved, what will become of the ungodly and the sinner? (4:18). Peter quotes the Greek translation of Proverbs 11:31 (which differs significantly from the Hebrew) to use Scripture for what he said in the previous verse.

Commit themselves to their faithful Creator (4:19). While this is the only New Testament place in which God is called "Creator" (a central teaching of the Old Testament), Jesus himself viewed God's creative activity as evidence that he could be trusted (Matt. 6:25–33; 10:29–31). More important, this passage in 1 Peter echoes Psalm 31:5: "Into your hands I commit my spirit; redeem me, O LORD, the God of truth." Jesus in his greatest persecution used a phrase from this verse in Luke 23:46.

The elders among you (5:1). The typical Jewish community, whether a village or a synagogue, was led by elders—honorable senior members of the community (one could be an older member of the community but lack honor because of shameful behavior at some time in one's life). Many pagan communities were also led by the senior members, whether one thinks of the *pater familas* (senior adult male, normally the father or elder brother of the other adult males) running the Roman family or village councils. The early church adopted the Jewish structure (e.g., Acts 11:30; 14:23; 15:2). Generally the elders or overseers (an alternative term, indicating function rather than seniority) led a city-wide church, irrespective of the number of house churches within the area. For example, Jerusalem had many house churches to accommodate the large number of believers, but we never read of more than one body of elders. Likewise Philippians 1:1 points to one group of leaders in a mature church. Titus 1:5 instructs Titus to appoint elders in every town, without any indication he should appoint multiple groups if the town was large. This structure is probably the reason the local bishop (in the second century) developed before the local church pastor (in the sixth century).

Peter assumes that the churches he is writing to are led by elders. While in 1:1

REFLECTIONS

FIRST-CENTURY CHRISTIANS COULD "REJOICE" DESPITE persecution because of their strong belief in the return of Christ and coming reward. Christians today appear focused on present happiness and success as a result of being Christian. Therefore there is a reluctance to take risks. What would it take to return to the church, not just a doctrine about the future, but a living expectation of the future strong enough to die for?

he has called himself an apostle, here he terms himself "a fellow elder," that is, a person who like them must lead the church.

Be shepherds of God's flock . . . serving as overseers (5:2). The image of the shepherd for the leaders of God's people goes back to the Old Testament. In Ezekiel 34 it applies to leaders who have failed, when God says, "Prophesy against the shepherds of Israel" (Ezek. 34:2). Yet the Jews always remembered that Moses and David were shepherds before they were chosen to lead Israel. These two became the image of the faithful leader, modeled on that of God ("The LORD is my shepherd" [Ps. 23:1]). The elders are to walk in this tradition, overseeing the "flock" (we notice that the "overseer" function is clearly indicated).

Because you are willing (5:2). The elder could easily feel he had to take up the office because he was the senior person in the community, but he might resent it because of its duties and because it exposed him to greater persecution.

Not greedy for money (5:2). Because the elders normally were not paid but still had oversight over the charity funds, an attitude of service rather than a desire for money was imperative. First Timothy 5:17–18 teaches that some elders should be paid (the Greek term for "honor" can also mean "pay" [cf. the English "honorarium"]; "double" in biblical literature often means "full," thus "full pay"). Yet even if that were sometimes the norm for certain elders throughout the church, the part-time elders in many areas would have continued unpaid.

Not lording it over those entrusted to you (5:3). The models of leadership in the Roman world were those of hierarchical structure in which the leaders gave orders and those under them obeyed (as Jesus notes in Mark 10:42 and the centurion states in Matt. 8:9). Peter rejects this hierarchical model and instead instructs the elders to be "examples to the flock," leading by modeling rather than by commanding. This fits the picture of the Palestinian shepherd walking in front of the flock and calling the sheep to come after him or her.

Chief Shepherd (5:4). This title for Jesus is taken from the picture of God in Psalm 23 as well as from sayings of Jesus, such as those in John 10 (e.g., "I am the good shepherd," 10:11).

SHEPHERD

A modern Syrian shepherd with his sheep.

Crown of glory (5:4). This Chief Shepherd returns as an official with high authority. That is, one would expect the Chief Shepherd to give wages to his undershepherds, and "will receive" *is* the language for receiving wages. But this Chief Shepherd gives for wages what a high official might give, "the crown of glory," such as was given to the victorious general after a battle (e.g., to wear in a triumphal procession, when such an honor was granted to him) or the winning athletes in the games. Those crowns, however, were laurel leaves and would fade. The crown for the elders will never fade, so is perhaps thought of as made of a precious metal.

Young men ... be submissive to those who are older (5:5). Submission was an appropriate cultural virtue that all segments of the culture would have approved of. In this case, however, it fits the situation of persecution, for younger men, especially if unmarried, tend to be more radical and in a tense situation need to listen to the seasoned wisdom of the elders.

Humility toward one another (5:5). This command is based on Proverbs 3:34, which is also quoted in a similar context in James 4:6–10. It broadens the submission to the whole community and not only preserves the internal unity of the church, but it is also the basis for the proper response to persecution.

Cast all your anxiety on him (5:7). This instruction may be based on teachings of Jesus, such as Matthew 6:25–34: If God cares for the birds and clothes the lilies, what is the Christian worrying about? The teaching is another that fits well in the situation of persecution.

"LIKE A ROARING LION. . ."

Be self-controlled and alert (5:8). First Peter has twice before called for self-control (1:13; 4:7), a virtue valued in his world. Now he combines it with being "alert," a term referring to a soldier on watch. Jesus used this word for alertness as the end approaches.[32]

Your enemy the devil prowls around like a roaring lion looking for someone to devour (5:8). The term "the devil" is Greek for "accuser" and the equivalent for the Hebrew "Satan." While the Old Testament has relatively little to say about the devil (and only speaks of him by name in the later books), intertestamental Judaism was well aware of him, as is the New Testament.[33] Job 1:7 speaks of the devil roaming around, while the picture of a roaring lion comes from Psalm 22:13. "Devour" refers to swallowing in one gulp, as the fish did to Jonah. Certainly this picture presents a good reason to be alert!

Resist him, standing firm in the faith (5:9). This was apparently a common teaching in the church. In James 4:7, as here, one is to "resist" the devil. In James the means of resistance are not noted, but here they are clearly stated. The devil devours by getting a person to renounce or compromise his or her faith; standing firm in one's commitment is an act of resistance.

Restore you and make you strong, firm and steadfast (5:10). Restoration has to do with the production of character; "strong" means strong in faith, underlined by the rare word "firm." The final word, "steadfast," means "placed on a solid foundation."

To him be the power for ever and ever. Amen (5:11). This is an abbreviation of the doxology in 4:11. The final "Amen" is an untranslated Aramaic or Hebrew word meaning "sure," which along with other untranslated expressions like "Hallelujah" and "Maranatha" have passed into the church's liturgical language. "Amen" is a response something like "Yes!" or "So be it!"

Letter Closing (5:12–14)

With the help of Silas (5:12). Having finished the letter body, Peter comes to the letter closing. It is equivalent to the salutation and signature of an English letter. It is at this point that a *Greek* author often took the stylus himself, making the last paragraph or two visibly different from the careful scribal hand that preceded it. Even if Silas or someone else wrote the whole letter, stylistically it was important to indicate the closing as if you were writing it yourself. The first item in the closing identifies the letter carrier, who in this case may have been virtually the cowriter. In Romans 16:22 Paul allows the scribe Tertius to identify himself, but here Peter uses the formula that identifies the letter carrier,[34] adding that Silas is a "faithful brother." This should remove any doubts readers might have had about the role Silas has played while with Peter or any questions about the expansion he might give as the person carrying the letter. (The person carrying a letter like this one was expected to give an oral expansion along with reading the letter.) Saying he is a "faithful brother" identifies him as one who shared Peter's ministry.

Briefly (5:12). Saying that he had written "briefly" is more a statement of politeness than one of fact. Ancient letters were supposed to be brief, so even Hebrews claims to be brief (Heb. 13:22).

Encouraging you and testifying that this is the true grace of God. Stand fast in it (5:12). This clause states the purpose of the letter (another part of a proper Greek letter closing).

She who is in Babylon . . . Mark (5:13). This next part of the letter closing is the greetings. In many cultures travelers with letters are expected to bring greetings from friends and relatives in a distant location; it would be impolite not to do so. "She who is in Babylon" and "Mark" could indicate Peter's wife and literal son, since we know that he sometimes traveled with a wife (1 Cor. 9:5) and could easily have had an adult son by this time (Peter was already married in Mark 1:30, around thirty years earlier). However, these two expressions probably indicate the church (the Greek word for "church" is feminine, thus "she") in Rome (Babylon equals Rome in Rev. 17:5, 9) and John Mark of Jerusalem (Acts 12:12). Mark was Paul's companion in travel (Acts 13:5), whom Paul calls for at the end of his life (2 Tim. 4:11). The reason

REFLECTIONS

PETER EXPECTS CHRISTIANS TO DEMONSTRATE BY their lifestyle that they are family. It has fathers (the elders) and youths, family issues and family affection. Today we often contrast family with church rather than finding family in the church. Perhaps we should consider how we might demonstrate in our estranged and divorcing age that the church is a family that will never reject its members and never break up through divorce or death.

for suspecting this is the meaning is not only that the church in 2 John 1 is called "the chosen lady," but also that otherwise the letter would lack a greeting from the church in Peter's location, which would be a strange oversight. Also, there is no other indication that Peter had a physical son named "Mark."

Kiss of love (5:14). The standard Greco-Roman family greeting was a kiss on each cheek, mentioned repeatedly in the New Testament (e.g., Rom. 16:16). While it was sometimes exchanged between rulers and clients, it was normally only used within a family. Thus Christian brothers and sisters were indicating by its use that they considered one another not just members of a club, but family. This practice may well have been the source of the rumor that the love among Christian brothers and sisters was physical, not simply an emotional bond.[35] While the practice was later confined to the Eucharist, in the first century it was probably used for greeting and parting.

Peace (5:14). This final benediction is Greek for the Hebrew *shalom* (see comments on 1:2). It fits the situation of persecution well.

ANNOTATED BIBLIOGRAPHY

Balch, David L. *Let Wives Be Submissive: The Domestic Code in 1 Peter.* SBLMS, 26. Atlanta: Scholars, 1981.

A specific study of 1 Peter 2–3, which remains a starting point for the study of such codes.

Davids, Peter H. *The First Epistle of Peter.* NICNT. Eerdmans, 1990.

An expansion of the material found in this commentary, along with extensive introductory materials.

Elliott, John H. *A Home for the Homeless.* Minneapolis: Fortress, 1981.

The first major work on 1 Peter to set it in the context of the social values of his world. While not perfect, it is a groundbreaking work.

Kelly, J. N. D. *The Epistles of Peter and of Jude.* London: Adam and Charles Black, 1976.

The major conservative work on 1 Peter between Selwyn and Michaels; still very useful.

Marshall, I. Howard. *1 Peter.* IVPNTC. Downers Grove: InterVarsity, 1991.

The best of the brief commentaries on 1 Peter; by a leading evangelical scholar.

Michaels, J. Ramsey. *1 Peter.* WBC 49. Waco, Tex.: Word, 1988.

A major evangelical commentary on 1 Peter based on the Greek text and including exposition.

Selwyn, Edward Gordon. *The First Epistle of St. Peter.* London: Macmillan, 1969.

A careful study of the Greek text, to which all other commentators refer.

CHAPTER NOTES

Main Text Notes

1. 1 Peter 1:14, 18; 2:9–10, 25; 3:6; 4:3–4.
2. Pliny, *Letters* 10.96.
3. For more information on the mystery religions see E. Ferguson, "Religions, Graeco-Roman," *DLNT*, 1006–11; M. W. Myer, *The Ancient Mysteries: A Sourcebook* (San Francisco: Harper, 1987).
4. E.g., Deut. 33:29; Ps. 3:3; 7:10; 18:2.
5. The resurrection of the dead and the rule of Jesus are the ultimate expressions of physical and political salvation, but the church saw signs of this ultimate salvation in the healing of the sick (physical), the Christian community (political), and the expulsion of demons (spiritual), partial and temporary though they were.
6. Cf. Rom. 8:24; Eph. 2:5, 8.

7. Cf. Acts 2:47; 1 Cor. 1:18; 2 Cor. 2:15.
8. Cf. Matt. 10:22; Rom. 5:9–10; 1 Tim. 4:16.
9. P. H. Davids, "Suffering in 1 Peter and the New Testament," in idem, *The First Epistle of Peter* (NICNT; Grand Rapids: Eerdmans, 1990), 30–44.
10. E.g., Matt. 6:25; 10:39; Acts 27:10.
11. Robert L. Webb, *John the Baptizer and Prophet* (Sheffield: Sheffield Academic Press, 1991), esp. ch. 1.
12. J. M. Reese, "Obedience," in J. J. Pilch and B. J. Malina, *Biblical Social Values and Their Meaning* (Peabody, Mass.: Hendrickson, 1993), 125–26.
13. J. J. Pilch, "Parenting" in Pilch and Malina, ibid., 128–31.
14. A. A. Ruprecht, "Slave, Slavery," *DPL*, 881–83; S. S. Bartchy, "Slave, Slavery," *DLNT*, 1098–1102.
15. See, for example, Rev. 1:6; 5:10; 20:6.
16. M. Reasoner, "Emperor, Emperor Cult," *DLNT*, 321–26.
17. B. Rapske, "Christians and the Roman Empire," *DLNT*, 1059–63.
18. M. Hengel, *Crucifixion* (Philadelphia: Fortress, 1977).
19. Philo, *Virtues* 39; *Moses* 2.243; Plutarch, *Mor.* 1 and 141.
20. For Seneca see *De Ben.* 7.9.
21. Epictetus as quoted in *Encheiridion* 40.
22. For example, see Plutarch, *Praec. Conj.* 45.
23. For example, the Jew Philo, *Drunkenness* 55, and the pagan Plato, *Resp.* 5.455e, both observe that women were physically weaker than men.
24. For example, see Deut. 10:18; Ps. 68:5; 146:9; Jer. 49:11; Mal. 3:5.
25. The Masoretic text has "the Lord Almighty" (*Yahweh Sabaoth*), while the Septuagint has "the Lord himself" (*kyrion auton*). First Peter has "the Lord Christ" (*kyrion ton Christon*).
26. For instance, Tacitus, *Ann.* 15.44.3 calls Christians, "a class hated for their abominations." He notes in 15.44.5 that they were convicted of "hatred of the human race [*odium humani generis*]," the same charge that magicians were charged with.
27. E.g., Gen. 19:1–3; Judg. 19:15–21.
28. For Jewish interpretation see the evidence presented in P. H. Davids, "Tradition and Citation in the Epistle of James," in W. W. Gasque and W. S. LaSor, eds., *Scripture, Tradition and Interpretation* (Grand Rapids: Eerdmans, 1978), 113–16.
29. Barth L. Campbell, *Honor, Shame, and the Rhetoric of 1 Peter* (SBLDS 160; Atlanta: Scholars, 1998), 196–97.
30. E.g., Rom. 11:36; 16:27; 1 Tim. 1:17; 6:16; 2 Tim. 4:18; Heb. 13:21; 2 Peter 3:18, all of which have similar wording to this text in 1 Peter.
31. Tacitus, *An.*15.44.5–7 from J. Stevenson, *A New Eusebius*.
32. Matt. 24:42–43; 25:13; 26:38–41.
33. Two excellent books on this topic are Sydney H. T. Page, *The Powers of Evil: A Biblical Study of Satan and Demons* (Grand Rapids: Baker, 1995); Stephen F. Noll, *Angels of Light, Powers of Darkness* (Downers Grove: InterVarsity, 1998).
34. Randolph Richards, "Theological Bias in Interpreting διὰ Σιλουανοῦ . . . ἔγραψα in 1 Pet. 5:12," a paper read at the 1999 meeting of the Evangelical Theological Society in Danvers, Mass.
35. G. Stählin, "φιλέω," *TDNT*, 9:118–24, 138–46. The erotic kiss is not stressed in Greco-Roman literature, although if one treated an unrelated male or female as if they were family, it might be assumed that one was treating them as husband or wife. See Robert Banks, *Going to Church in the First Century* (Chipping Norton, NSW, Australia), 12–15, 39, for an illustration of this practice.

Sidebar and Chart Notes

A-1. Eph. 5:21–6:9; Col. 3:18–4:1.

A-2. See further Dale W. Brown, "Revolutionary Subordination: A Bible Study of the Haustafeln," *BLT* 20 (1975): 159–64; Eric C. Lovik, "A Look at the Ancient House Codes and Their Contributions to Understanding 1 Peter 3:1–7," *CBTJ* 11 (1995): 49–63; John Howard Yoder, *The Politics of Jesus* (Grand Rapids: Eerdmans, 1994).

A-3. For example, *2 En.* 7:1, "And those men picked me up and brought me up to the second heaven. And they showed me, and I saw a darkness greater than earthly darkness. And there I perceived prisoners under guard. . . ." Later in the chapter the prisoners are identified as the fallen angels.

A-4. See further M. Reasoner, "Persecution," *DLNT*, 907–14.

A-5. See further: Pilch and Malina, *Biblical Social Values and Their Meaning*, and David deSilva, *Despising Shame: Honor Discourse and Community Maintenance in Hebrews* (Atlanta: Scholars, 1995).

2 PETER

by Douglas J. Moo

Authorship

The writer of the letter identifies himself clearly: "Simon Peter, a servant and apostle of Jesus Christ" (1:1). Some scholars doubt the accuracy of this identification, arguing that certain indications from within the letter reveal that Peter the apostle could not have written it. But these arguments are not convincing.[1] If, then, Peter did write the letter, what can we learn about his own situation at the time? In a phrase, not much. Peter, of course, appears as a prominent figure throughout the Gospels and in the early chapters of the book of Acts. He was a key leader in the early church in Jerusalem. Persecution, however, forced him to flee Palestine; Luke tells us vaguely that he "left for another place" (Acts 12:17). What this "other place" may have been has been a topic of lively conjecture.

While we cannot be sure where Peter fled after his release from imprisonment, we do find him back in Jerusalem some years later for the council held there (Acts 15). Paul's references to "Cephas" (= Peter) in

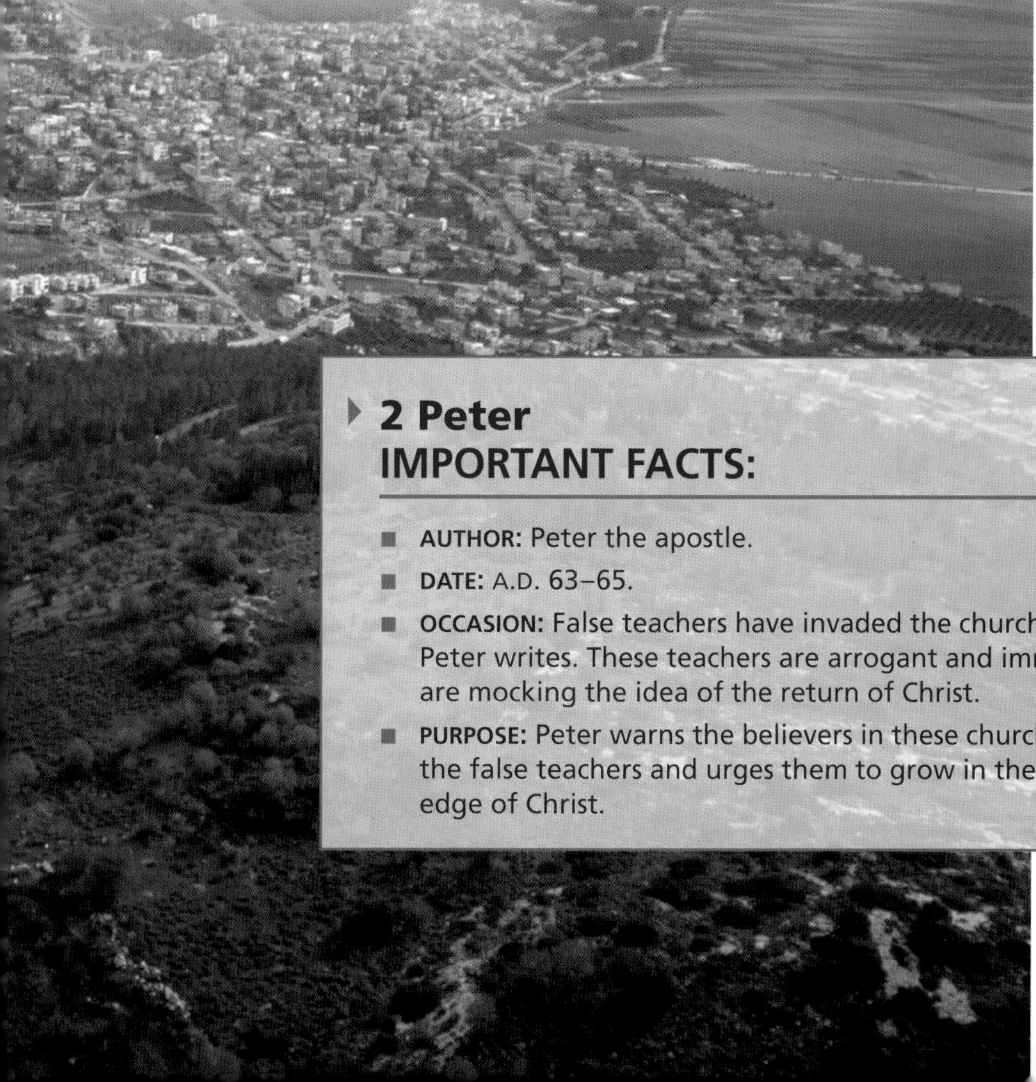

MOUNT TABOR

Traditional site of the transfiguration of Jesus.

2 Peter IMPORTANT FACTS:

- **AUTHOR:** Peter the apostle.
- **DATE:** A.D. 63–65.
- **OCCASION:** False teachers have invaded the churches to which Peter writes. These teachers are arrogant and immoral and are mocking the idea of the return of Christ.
- **PURPOSE:** Peter warns the believers in these churches about the false teachers and urges them to grow in their knowledge of Christ.

1 Corinthians suggest that he may have ministered in Corinth for a time (1 Cor. 1:12; 9:5). Nothing more is known about Peter until he writes a letter from Rome about A.D. 60 to Christians in northern Asia Minor (see the introduction to 1 Peter). We have only later legends to go by in reconstructing the last years of Peter. Tradition confirms that he spent some time in Rome.[2] Apparently reliable testimony has it that Peter, along with Paul, perished in the persecution of Emperor Nero in Rome in A.D. 64–65.[3] Some traditions hold that he was crucified head downward, but they do not appear to be reliable.[4]

The style and teaching of 2 Peter suggest strongly that it was written toward the end of Peter's life. It must have been written after A.D. 60 or so if 2 Peter 3:1 is a reference to 1 Peter. Peter was in Rome, as we have seen, in A.D. 60, and again at the time of his death in A.D. 64–65. He may have been there also when he wrote 2 Peter, therefore, although we cannot be sure. Nor can we be sure of the location of the Christians Peter addresses. Again, if the earlier letter implied in 2 Peter 3:1 is 1 Peter, then we can also know that 2 Peter is addressed to the same churches in northern Asia Minor. We are left with more questions than answers in our quest for specifics about the situation in which 2 Peter was written.

The False Teachers

Peter tells us little about what the false teachers are actually teaching. His only clear reference is to their "scoffing" about the return of Christ to judge the world (3:3–4). He spends most of the letter

TRAVELS OF PETER

From Judea to Asia Minor to Greece to Rome.

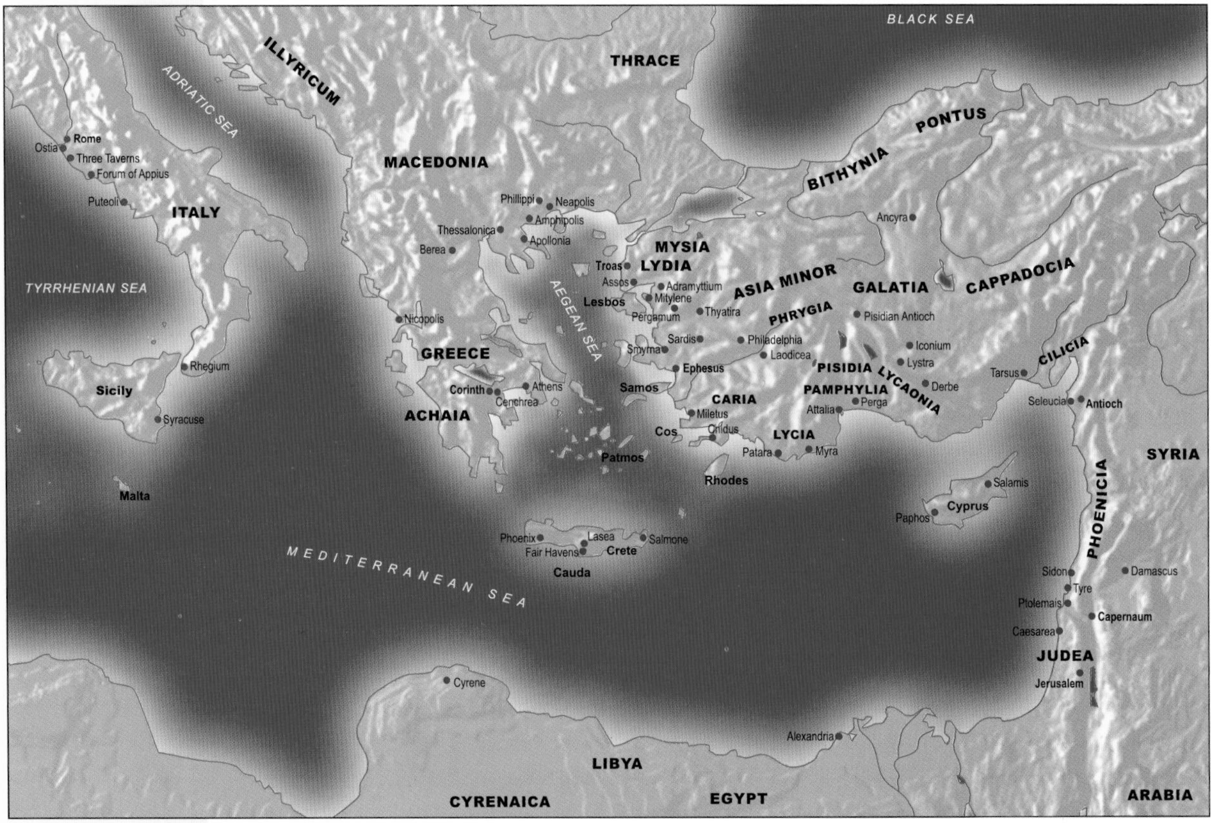

denouncing their lifestyle. They assume that the grace of God gives them the liberty to do just about anything they want (2:19–20). This "libertinism" manifests itself in arrogance toward authority (2:10–11), sexual misconduct (perhaps including homosexuality), excess in drinking and eating, and greed for money (2:13–16, 18–20).

Unfortunately, this profile is not specific enough to enable us to identify the false teachers with any known first-century group. Many scholars think that the teaching may have some relationship to Gnosticism. Although not formally distinguished as a full-blown "ism" until the second century, gnostic-like ideas were in circulation throughout the last half of the first century. Among other things, gnostics tended rigidly to separate the material from the spiritual realm. What people did in the "body," therefore, had little to do with spirituality: Note the libertine lifestyle Peter describes in chapter 2.[5]

But just how difficult it is to pin down these false teachers is revealed in the very different proposal of Jerome Neyrey. He notes that one of the most influential Greco-Roman philosophies of the day was Epicureanism. The Epicureans were known especially for their denial of providence, the afterlife, or any kind of divine judgment—just the view that seems to be taken by the false teachers according to chapter 3. In contrast to the popular picture of Epicureans, they did not foster a licentious lifestyle. But their denial of providence and the activity of the gods in daily life could easily lead among some adherents to such a lifestyle. This is just the point made by the early Christian writer Lactantius:

> If any chieftan or pirates or leaders of robbers were exhorting his men to acts of violence, what other language could he employ than to say the same things which Epicurus says: that the gods take no notice; that they are not affected with anger or kind feeling; that the punishment of a future state is not to be dreaded, because the souls die after death, and there is no future state of punishment at all. (*Inst.* 3.17)[6]

These conflicting proposals suggest that we do not have enough evidence to identify the false teachers that lie behind 2 Peter. Indeed, our very quest to identify them with a particular group may be misguided. People in the ancient world, as in our day, were bombarded by viewpoints and ideas from many different perspectives. They could probably not have themselves always distinguished the exact religious or philosophical sources for their ultimate beliefs and habits of life. The false teachers, in other words, may have been influenced both by the broad philosophical climate of Epicureanism as well as incipient Gnosticism—and by other movements as well.

The Letter

Peter writes moral instruction to believers just before his death (1:14). This scenario is similar to that found in a popular Jewish intertestamental genre called a *testament*. Works such as the *Testaments of the Twelve Patriarchs*, the *Testament of Job*, and the *Testament of Moses* illustrate the genre. The original impetus for the form comes from Jacob's words to his sons on his deathbed in Genesis 48:8–49:27. Jewish writers used it as a convenient device to convey moral advice. Many scholars think that 2 Peter is in the form of a testament. Since such testaments are usually pseudonymous (i.e., written in someone else's name), these same scholars also think 2 Peter is pseudonymous.

They suggest that a disciple of Peter has built a letter of moral encouragement on the basis of some genuine fragments of Peter's own teaching.[7] However, while similarities between 2 Peter and the Jewish testaments exist—and Peter may well have adapted it to his own purposes—2 Peter in genre is a letter, not a testament. We do not have evidence that letters were written pseudonymously.

Introduction (1:1–2)

In common with both secular and New Testament letters, Peter identifies himself as the sender of the letter and then identifies his readers. They, however, are described in general, theological terms, leaving us in doubt about where they lived.

A servant . . . of Jesus Christ (1:1). The title, of course, connotes Peter's humble recognition that Jesus Christ is his Lord and that he is obliged to serve him in any way the Lord might decide. This was what it meant to be a "servant" or "slave" (*doulos*). But great figures in Israel's past were also called "servants" of God, especially Moses (e.g., Josh. 14:7; 2 Kings 18:12) and David (e.g., Ps. 18:1; Ezek. 34:23). So the title also conveys a certain honor and authority.

The Need to Grow in Knowledge of Christ (1:3–11)

This paragraph gets right to the heart of Peter's concern for his readers. He reminds them that God has provided all that is needed to become spiritually mature, and that believers thus have the responsibility to use the immense resources at their disposal to grow in relationship to Christ and thus secure their welcome in the kingdom of God.

Knowledge (1:3). Peter highlights the importance of "knowledge" throughout his letter (cf. 1:5, 6, 8; 2:20; 3:18). But especially significant is the way he ends the letter: "Therefore, dear friends, since you already know this, be on your guard so that you may not be carried away by the error of lawless men and fall from your secure position. But grow in the grace and

PETER'S HOME IN CAPERNAUM

The modern structure is built over the site identified as the home of Peter.

knowledge of our Lord and Savior Jesus Christ. To him be glory both now and forever! Amen" (3:17–18). By focusing on "knowledge" at both the beginning and the end of the letter, Peter draws special attention to it. The "framing" of material by beginning and ending on the same note is called *inclusio* and is used widely throughout the New Testament.

We are less certain why Peter highlights knowledge in this way. One possibility is that he is implicitly correcting the false teachers by using a term that they themselves put great stock in and setting it in its appropriate Christian context. As we noted in the introduction, many scholars think that Peter may be combating some form of early or incipient "Gnosticism," a religious system that focused on intellectual knowledge (Gk. *gnōsis*). While we cannot be certain that Peter is combatting early gnostics, we can surmise that these teachers are singling out *gnōsis* in a way that the later gnostics also did and that he therefore wants to help his readers understand that useful religious knowledge is always focused on God in Christ and has a thoroughly practical purpose: conformity to the image of Christ.

You may participate in the divine nature and escape the corruption in the world (1:4). The language Peter uses here is unusual in the Bible and is reminiscent of the pantheistic focus of some ancient Near Eastern and Greco-Roman religions. These religions had a mystical bent, promising deliverance from the contagion of the material world through absorption into the person of a god. The mystery religions, for instance, offered initiates the opportunity to become identified with a god and so escape death and corruption.[8] Philo, a Jewish philosopher from Alexandria, uses some of the same language Peter here uses in just this sense:

> For how could the soul have conceived of God, had he not breathed into it and mightily laid hold of it? For the mind of man would never have ventured to soar so high so as to grasp the nature of God, had not God himself drawn it up to himself, so far as it was possible that the mind of man should be drawn up, and stamped it with the impress of the powers that are within the scope of its understanding.[9]

However, while Peter probably borrows the language from this cultural context, he applies it to a different conception. "Participating in the divine nature" means not to become absorbed in a mystical union with a god, but to the indwelling of God's Spirit and the consequent holiness of life that arises from that indwelling. We participate in the divine nature by imitating in our thinking and behaving the holy character of God himself.

Add to your faith goodness; and to goodness, knowledge . . . (1:5–7). The series of moral virtues in these verses resembles an ancient literary style called the *sorites.* An example from Jewish writings comes in Wisdom 6:17–20:[10]

> *The beginning of wisdom is the most*
> *sincere desire for instruction,*
> *and concern for instruction is love*
> *of her,*
> *and love of her is the keeping*
> *of her laws,*
> *and giving heed to her laws is*
> *assurance of immortality,*
> *and immortality brings one near*
> *to God;*
> *so the desire for wisdom leads to*
> *a kingdom.*

One implication of recognizing this literary device in 2 Peter 1:5–7 is the possibility that Peter is not suggesting that the virtues he lists must always be acquired in the order in which he lists them. Indeed, it is unlikely that he thinks believers can truly acquire "goodness" before "knowledge," since knowing God is basic to all virtues.

Self-control (1:6). Peter's mention of this virtue (Gk. *enkrateia*) is another example of his "accomodation" to Hellenistic culture. This virtue was prized by Greco-Roman philosophers as a basic necessity for a thoughtful and intelligent person. Aristotle and Philo made a great deal of this virtue.[11]

Holding Fast to the Biblical Promises (1:12–21)

In 1:12–15, Peter focuses on his own situation as a way of giving greater impetus to his exhortations. He then turns to what seems to be the key doctrinal problem with the false teachers: their scorn of the idea of Christ's return in glory. Peter emphasizes the certainty of that return by reminding them of the Transfiguration, a prefigurement of Christ's eschatological glory, and by insisting that the prophecies about that return are certain to be fulfilled.

The tent of this body (1:13). There is no word corresponding to "body" in the Greek text here; the NIV has added it to clarify the meaning of "tent." The relationship between these words is therefore one of definition; we could paraphrase "this tent, that is, my body." Greek authors sometimes use the word "tent" (*skēnōma*) to refer to the physical body, especially when wanting to distinguish it from the soul, or spirit, of a person. Paul uses a related term (*skēnos*) in just this way: "Now we know that if the earthly tent we live in is destroyed, we have a building from God, an eternal house in heaven, not built by human hands. . . . For while we are in this tent, we groan . . ." (2 Cor. 5:1, 4a). The word is appropriate in this context, where Peter is thinking of the day when he will "put . . . aside" this tent.

I will soon put it aside (1:14). The language Peter uses here to describe his death is yet another case of contextualization. His language of "putting aside" the body might suggest that he agrees with the Greek notion of the immortality of the soul. But Peter hints at his belief in the usual biblical teaching about resurrection in his first letter (1 Peter 4:6; cf. 3:18). So we can presume that Peter here adapts a normal Greek way of speaking about death without taking over the Greek notion of immortality.

REFLECTIONS

PETER'S CLAIM THAT BELIEVERS MUST ACTIVELY cultivate spiritual virtues in order "to make your calling and election sure" is controversial, especially for Calvinists,who teach what is called "unconditional election": God chooses from eternity past who will be saved; and his choice is final and irrevocable. How, then, can believers add anything to God's sovereign choice? Arminians, of course, respond that this verse (along with many others) reveals that God's choosing takes place in conjunction with our own choosing to respond to the gospel of Jesus Christ. But the Calvinist view can be maintained if we recognize that God's sovereign choosing of us always demands our response to it. The Bible suggests a careful balance, or tension, between God's sovereignty and our own responsibility. God chooses, but we must choose also. God brings us to final salvation; but we are responsible to act on the basis of his grace in order to reach that final goal.

▸ Views of the Afterlife

The Greeks had a variety of views on the afterlife. Adherents to the Orphic religions thought of death as a time when the soul would be released from the body to enjoy an immortal existence. Both Plato and Aristotle held that some part of the human being (whether the "soul" or "reason") was immortal and would live on after death. But probably the dominant view was that found in Homer—that most people (apart from notorious sinners and great heroes) would survive death only as bodiless shades in Hades, without consciousness of personal existence.[A-1]

The biblical perspective is quite different. Hinted at in the Old Testament and made explicit in the New Testament, biblical authors teach that the body will be raised from the dead to live forever. Not all Jews in the intertestamental period, however, agreed; some taught the immortality of the soul.

As the Lord Jesus Christ has made clear to me (1:14). Some scholars who think that an anonymous Christian wrote 2 Peter after his death assert that the author is here referring to the famous *Quo Vadis* legend. This legend is found in the apocryphal *Acts of Peter* and tells how Peter, on leaving Rome to escape arrest, is confronted by Jesus. Peter asks the Lord, "Where are you going" [Lat. *Quo vadis*]; the Lord responds that he is going to Rome to be crucified. Peter then turns back to be crucified in Rome. But we certainly do not need to refer to this legend to explain Peter's reference, for Jesus predicted Peter's death during his postresurrection appearances: "'I tell you the truth, when you were younger you dressed yourself and went where you wanted; but when you are old you will stretch out your hands, and someone else will dress you and lead you where you do not want to go.' Jesus said this to indicate the kind of death by which Peter would glorify God" (John 21:18–19). To be sure, this prophecy gives no indication of timing. But we can surmise that Peter writes 2 Peter in a situation where intense persecution has broken out; he might even be under arrest. So he now realizes that the Lord's prediction of his martyr's death is about to be fulfilled.

We did not follow cleverly invented stories (1:16). "Stories" translates the word *mythoi*, literally, "myths." This word was used in a wide variety of ways in the ancient world, but the meaning that best fits the context is "fictional account, fable."[12] The *mythos* was often viewed as a mechanism to teach religious truth to people who did not have the intellectual capacity to apprehend matters of the spirit directly. Aristotle comments: "The mythical form is chosen to make apprehension possible for the masses, for their religious and ethical instruction."[13] We can assume that the false teachers are claiming that the idea of Jesus' return in glory was just such a *mythos*—a religious story to encourage "ordinary" Christians.

The power and coming of our Lord Jesus Christ (1:16). "Power" and "coming" form a construction that means "powerful coming." The word behind "coming" is the familiar *parousia*, used throughout the New Testament to denote the second "coming" of Jesus. The word has the basic sense of "presence" or "arrival." Some of the Greeks used it to refer to the special "presence" or even "coming" of a god. Jewish writers, accordingly, applied the word to the biblical God: Josephus, for instance, uses it to depict the terrifying appearance of God at Sinai.[14]

"This is my Son, whom I love; with him I am well pleased" (1:17). These words of God himself at the occasion of the Transfiguration allude to two important Old Testament passages. The first is Psalm 2:7, where God addresses the messianic king; the second is Isaiah 42:1, the opening of the first Servant Song in Isaiah. These words, therefore, combine to identify Jesus as the Messiah, whose mission will take the form of the Suffering Servant of Isaiah.

The sacred mountain (1:18). This language is again cited by some who doubt that Peter could have written this letter. They claim that it smacks of a later period in Christian history, when the places where significant events in the life of Jesus took place were being revered as "holy" places. But such skepticism is unwarranted. As R. Bauckham has pointed out, Peter is probably alluding to Psalm 2:6 (note that Ps. 2:7 is alluded to in 2 Peter 1:17): "I have installed my King on Zion, my holy hill."[15]

Until the day dawns (1:19). The rich biblical teaching about the "Day of the Lord" makes it certain that Peter intends here more than a metaphor. The "Day of the Lord" is the day when God visits his people for judgment or salvation (Deut. 30:17–18), and the prophets use the phrase extensively as a way of depicting the final events of human history (e.g., Joel 1:15; Obad. 15).[16]

And the morning star rises in your hearts (1:19). "Morning star" translates a word that means, literally, "light-bringer" (*phōsphoros*). Ancient people thought especially of the planet Venus as the "light-bringer," since it often appears just before the dawn. Peter picks up this pop-

MOUNT TABOR

Traditional site of the transfiguration of Jesus.

ular imagery to describe the effect of the coming of the Day of the Lord on the believer: The "morning star" rises in the heart. Behind Peter's imagery may also lie the biblical use of "star" language to depict the Messiah (Num. 24:17; cf. Rev. 22:16).

By the prophet's own interpretation (1:20). Some interpreters think that the verse should be translated: "No prophecy of Scripture is a matter of one's own interpretation." The focus would thus shift to the current interpretation of prophecy. But the interpretation assumed in the NIV is preferable. That Peter is referring to the prophet's own "interpretation" or "unravelling" (*epilysis*) is probable because the Old Testament uses this same language to speak of the interpretation of dreams sent by the Lord. See especially the story of Joseph's interpretation of the dreams of the baker and butler in Genesis 40–41.

Peter's insistence on this point may have arisen because the false teachers were making a contrary point. At a later date, for instance, the Ebionites (radical Jewish Christians) claimed that the prophets spoke "of their own intelligence and not the truth."[17]

Introduction of the False Teachers (2:1–3)

Peter now turns to the topic that will dominate the rest of the letter: the false teachers who are plaguing these Christians. The key note in these verses is destruction: their heresies are "destructive" (2:1), and the false teachers themselves are destined for "destruction" (2:1, 3).

There were also false prophets among the people (2:1). Peter reminds his readers that the Old Testament is strewn with examples of people who claimed to speak in the name of the Lord but were leading the people astray by propagating their own notions. As Richard Bauckham notes, these false prophets in Israel generally displayed three characteristics: (1) They did not speak with God's authority; (2) their message was usually upbeat, in contrast to the authentic prophets' warning of divine judgment; and (3) they were denounced as worthy of condemnation. Peter applies all three characteristics to the false teachers he denounces.

There will be false teachers among you (2:1). The word "false teachers" (*pseudodidaskaloi*) is used nowhere else in the New Testament, although Paul does warn about "teachers" who "say what [people's] itching ears want to hear" (2 Tim. 4:3; cf. also 1 Tim. 4:1). We might expect Peter to complete his comparison in verse 1 by announcing the coming of "false prophets" in the church, who were like the false prophets of old. Perhaps, however, the people introducing these doctrines do not claim to be prophets. Another surprising feature of this verse is the future tense Peter uses: "will be." Elsewhere in the letter Peter appears to presuppose that these false teachers have already arrived on the scene. Most likely Peter is thinking of Jesus' own prophecies about the rise of false teachers in the last days (see esp. Jesus' warnings in the Olivet Discourse):

> Jesus answered: "Watch out that no one deceives you. For many will come in my name, claiming, 'I am the Christ,' and will deceive many. . . .
>
> At that time many will turn away from the faith and will betray and

hate each other, and many false prophets will appear and deceive many people. . . .

At that time if anyone says to you, 'Look, here is the Christ!' or, 'There he is!' do not believe it. For false Christs and false prophets will appear and perform great signs and miracles to deceive even the elect—if that were possible.[18]

COLOSSEUM IN ROME

Outside and inside view (floor missing).

Since the early Christians believed they were living in "the last days," they could readily apply such predictions to their own circumstances.

The sovereign Lord (2:1). The Greek here is *despotēs* (from which we get "despot"), a term applied to God or Christ only four other times in the New Testament.[19] It connotes commanding authority, and Peter probably uses it to underscore the false teachers' rebellious attitudes. Their scorn of authority emerges at several points in 2 Peter 2.

Destructive heresies (2:1). The NIV rendering is quite literal; indeed, it is a transliteration—the Greek word is *haire-*

seis. But this translation may not be entirely accurate. In the New Testament period, this Greek word refers to a "party" or a "sect."[20] Only later did the word take on the sense of deviation from orthodox teaching.

Stories they have made up (2:3). This Greek expression was used in the classical period to denote deceitful speech; note *Testament of Reuben* 3:5, which refers to the person who "handles his affairs smoothly and secretly even with his relatives and household."

The Condemnation of the False Teachers (2:4–10a)

The end of the last paragraph (2:3) announces the theme of this one: "Their condemnation has long been hanging over them, and their destruction has not been sleeping." Peter cites Old Testament examples of God's judgment as warning to these false teachers. But he also encourages faithful Christians by reminding them that God also "knows how to rescue godly men from trials" (2:9).

God did not spare angels when they sinned (2:4). The examples of God's judgment that Peter cites in 2:5–6 are clear allusions to well-known Old Testament events: the flood of Noah and the destruction of Sodom and Gomorrah. But the reference in 2:4 is not so clear. Some interpreters think Peter may have in mind Isaiah 14:12–17 and Ezekiel 28:11–19. These texts may, according to some interpreters, refer to a primeval "fall" of Satan and the angels who followed him in his rebellion.[21] But it is not clear that Isaiah and Ezekiel are referring to such a fall. A more likely background emerges when we consider a prominent intertestamental Jewish tradition, which took its starting point from the enigmatic Genesis 6:1–4:

> When men began to increase in number on the earth and daughters were born to them, the sons of God saw that the daughters of men were beautiful, and they married any of them they chose. Then the LORD said, "My Spirit will not contend with man forever, for he is mortal; his days will be a hundred and twenty years."
>
> The Nephilim were on the earth in those days—and also afterward—when the sons of God went to the daughters of men and had children by them. They were the heroes of old, men of renown.

Old Testament scholars debate about whether the "sons of God" were human beings or angels; but the Jewish interpreters of Peter's day left no doubt about the matter. They viewed the "sons of God" as angels and their cohabiting with women as a key moment in the "fall" of the world into sin. The idea is found in several different books, but is most prominent in *1 Enoch*. See, for instance, 6:1–2:[22]

> In those days, when the children of man had multiplied, it happened that there were born unto them handsome and beautiful daughters. And the angels, the children of heaven, saw them and desired them, and they said to one another, "Come, let us choose wives for ourselves from among the daughters of man and beget us children."

Peter cites what was apparently a well-known tradition to illustrate the way in which God judges those who rebel against him.

Sent them to hell (2:4). These words translate a single Greek verb, *tartareō*. From this word comes "Tartarus," a common name for the subterranean abyss to which disobedient gods and rebellious people were consigned. Jewish writers had already adopted this term as a way of communicating in a Greek environment the biblical idea of a place of punishment for sin.[23] The NIV "hell" conveys the idea well enough but may miss one point. Tartarus was often pictured more as a temporary holding-place than a place of final punishment. Peter suggests that the angels who sinned are being "held for judgment."

Putting them into gloomy dungeons (2:4). This phrase continues to use popular Greek notions of the afterlife to convey the sense of judgment. It is not clear whether Peter is speaking of "gloomy dungeons" or "chains of darkness" (see the NIV footnote; the difference is a textual variant). But the idea of gloom and darkness conveys the sense of punishment. Note, for instance, *1 Enoch* 10:4: "Bind Azazel [a disobedient angel] hand and foot and throw him into darkness."

Noah, a preacher of righteousness (2:5). The Old Testament presumes that Noah, by his lifestyle and commitment to God's promise, was an example of righteousness in his generation. But it never calls him a "preacher." Intertestamental Jewish traditions, however, used this language for him.[24]

Condemned the cities of Sodom and Gomorrah (2:6). The destruction of the world through the Flood and the destruction by fire of Sodom and Gomorrah make a natural pair of examples of God's judgment. Nevertheless, Peter may be influenced by Jesus, who alluded to these two Old Testament incidents together:

> Just as it was in the days of Noah, so also will it be in the days of the Son of Man. People were eating, drinking, marrying and being given in marriage up to the day Noah entered the ark. Then the flood came and destroyed them all.
>
> It was the same in the days of Lot. People were eating and drinking, buying and selling, planting and building. But the day Lot left Sodom, fire and

SODOM

The salt pans south of Lisan—the possible site of Sodom.

sulfur rained down from heaven and destroyed them all. (Luke 17:26–29)

By burning them to ashes (2:6). The same Greek word that Peter uses here to denote the destruction of Sodom and Gomorrah (*tephroō*) was used by Dio Cassius to depict Pompeii after the eruption of Mount Vesuvius in A.D. 79 (Dio Cassius 46). Jewish authors used similar language to describe the fate of Sodom and Gomorrah. Philo claims that God "consumed the impious and their cities, and to the present day the memorials to the awful disaster are shewn in Syria, ruins and cinders and brimstone and smoke" (*Moses* 2.56).

Lot, a righteous man (2:7; cf. 2:8). This description of Lot is not out of keeping with the profile given in Genesis 19. Although vacillating in his faith to some extent, Lot, in the midst of a sinful context, never lost his basic orientation to God. Jewish writers before Peter also called him "righteous" (see, e.g., Wisd. Sol. 10:6: "Wisdom rescued a righteous man when the ungodly were perishing; he escaped the fire that descended on the Five Cities"). However, some other Jewish traditions portray Lot as a notorious sinner.

A Characterization of the False Teachers (2:10b–16)

Peter provides a profile of the false teachers' sinfulness by moving quickly through a list of their evil tendencies.

These men are not afraid to slander celestial beings (2:10). "Celestial beings" translates the Greek word *doxai* (lit., glories). The word could refer to illustrious or honored human beings, such as leaders in the early church. But a reference to angelic beings is more likely. To be sure the Old Testament never calls angels "glorious ones," but Jewish writers sometimes did. See, for example, *2 Enoch* 22:6–7: "And Michael, the Lord's leading angel, lifted me up and brought me in front of the face of the Lord. And the Lord said to his servants, sounding them out, 'Let Enoch join in and stand in front of my face forever! And the Lord's glorious ones did obeisance and said, 'Let Enoch yield in accordance with your word, O Lord!' "[25] Other Jewish traditions also link angels and glory.[26] The context further suggests that Peter refers to evil angels, since the "celestial beings" in this verse appear to be identical to the "beings" in 2 Peter 2:11, which the "angels" (apparently "good" angels) do not slander.

How are these false teachers slandering evil angels? Peter does not tell us; but perhaps their arrogance is manifesting itself in speaking in a disparaging way

REFLECTIONS

IN NO SPIRITUAL MATTER, PERHAPS, are Christians more prone to unfortunate extremes than in our attitude toward spiritual beings. Some believers tend virtually to ignore the entire spiritual realm, acting in practice as if the world of spirits does not exist. When this happens, we are open to the onslaughts of Satan. For his greatest victory, as C. S. Lewis reminds us, comes when people act as if he doesn't exist. But, in an overreaction to such neglect, some Christians go too far the other direction, giving too much credit to spiritual beings and failing to claim the benefits of Christ's victory over them at the cross.

about these beings. They may be dismissing the power and significance of the demons, willfully ignoring the degree to which their own actions are being influenced by them.

Angels . . . do not bring slanderous accusations against such beings (2:11). Nothing in the Old Testament directly supports this assertion; Peter is once again relying on Jewish tradition. Jude, in a roughly parallel text, quotes from a tradition found in *The Assumption of Moses* (cf. Jude 8–9); Peter may have the same text in mind. Or perhaps Peter continues to rely on *1 Enoch*. In chapter 9 of this book, the author describes how good angels, upon hearing the outcry of human beings as they are being harmed by evil angels, do not directly intervene but bring the matter before the Lord.

HADES

A statue of the underworld god.

They are like brute beasts, creatures of instinct, born only to be caught and destroyed (2:12). Peter alludes to a widespread ancient teaching about certain animals born only to be slaughtered and eaten.[27]

Their idea of pleasure is to carouse in broad daylight (2:13). The Greek for "pleasure" is *hēdonē*, from which we get the word "hedonist." The Greeks numbered this kind of "pleasure" among the four "deadly sins," sometimes contrasting it with "reason" (cf. the "unreasoning animals" of 2:12). Drinking and excessive eating in daylight hours were a standard indication of a degenerate lifestyle.[28]

Reveling in their pleasures while they feast with you (2:13). The allusion is probably to the "love feast," the meal that early Christians ate in conjunction with their celebration of the Lord's Supper. Such a meal is implied in 1 Corinthians 11:17–34 and is mentioned in many early Christian writings.[29]

With eyes full of adultery, they never stop sinning (2:14). Peter may be alluding to a popular ancient proverb, that a shameless man does not have *koras* (a pun, for the word can mean both "pupils" and "young women") in his eyes, but *pornas* ("prostitutes").[30]

They are experts in greed (2:14). "Experts" renders the Greek *gegymnasmenē*, a word that refers to athletic training. These false teachers, Peter implies, have worked hard to become as proficient in greediness as they are.

They have left the straight way and wandered off (2:15). The "way" was a popular means of characterizing a particular religious or philosophical teaching. The imagery is of a path that a true devotee will follow to the end. The Old Testament, therefore, pictures faithfulness to the Lord as a "straight path" to be followed, and the New Testament writers depict Christianity as a "Way."[31] Sin can therefore be described as "wandering" from that path. See, for example, God's warning to the people of Israel: "See, I am setting before you today a blessing and a curse—the blessing if you obey the commands of the LORD your God that I am giving you today; the curse if you disobey the commands of the LORD your God and turn from the way that I command you today by following other gods, which you have not known" (Deut. 11:26–28).

Balaam son of Beor (2:15). Balaam is introduced in Numbers 22–24 as a prophet whom the pagan king Balak pays to prophesy against Israel. Despite Balaam's own reluctance and corruption, God causes him to utter prophecies in favor of his people. Providing a point of connection between Numbers and 2 Peter is the use of the word "way" in the story. The "way of Balaam" in Numbers 22:23 is the road that Balaam is following; and in 22:32 Balaam is rebuked for taking a "reckless [way]." Peter's use of Balaam is undoubtedly influenced by the way he is used in Scripture as a negative example (Deut. 23:4–5).[32] The NIV's "son of Beor" either presumes a variant reading or simply standardizes the biblical names for Balaam's father. The best-attested text has "Bosor." This name may be a play on the Hebrew word for "flesh" (*basar*), reflecting Jewish traditions that characterize Balaam as a "fleshly" person.

Who loved the wages of wickedness (2:15). Hinted at in the Old Testament, Balaam's willingness to curse Israel for profit became a staple in Jewish stories about him.[33]

He was rebuked for his wrongdoing by a donkey . . .restrained the prophet's madness (2:16). Both are highlighted in Jewish traditions about Balaam. The idea of the donkey's "rebuke" of Balaam is found in several of the targums; and Philo calls Balaam "most foolish" of men.[34]

The False Teachers' Impact and Destiny (2:17–22)

If 2:10b–16 have focused on the false teachers' character, 2:17–22 stress their impact on other people. Because of the terrible spiritual effects of their teaching, their judgment will be certain and severe.

Springs without water (2:17). The dry Mediterranean climate, with long stretches of land and little water, rendered fresh water springs essential to life. As useless and dangerous as springs without water is the teaching of these false Christians.

Mists driven by a storm (2:17). Aristotle uses the rare Greek word translated "mist" here (*homichlē*) to refer to the haze left after the condensation of a cloud into rain.[35] Such condensation often dissipates and becomes the harbinger of dry weather.

They are worse off at the end than they were at the beginning (2:20). Peter probably alludes to Jesus' teaching at the end of his story about the evil spirit in Matthew 12:43–45:

When an evil spirit comes out of a man, it goes through arid places seeking rest and does not find it. Then it says, 'I will return to the house I left.' When it arrives, it finds the house unoccupied, swept clean and put in order. Then it goes and takes with it seven other spirits more wicked than itself, and they go in and live there. And the final condition of that man is worse than the first. That is how it will be with this wicked generation.

"A sow that is washed goes back to her wallowing in the mud" (2:22). The proverb that Peter quotes may go back to a popular seventh- or sixth-century B.C. book of proverbs called *Ahiqar*. The Aramaic version reads, in 8:8: "My son, you have been to me like the pig who went into the hot bath with people of quality, and when it came out of the hot bath, it saw a filthy hole and it went down and wallowed in it."[36]

Remembering the Truth (3:1–7)

After a chapter focused exclusively on the false teachers, Peter turns to his readers again. In contrast to the false teachers, who have forgotten the truth and lapsed into a heretical denial of the Lord's return, Peter wants his readers to "recall" what they have been taught by the prophets and by the Lord himself.

My second letter to you (3:1). With the New Testament canon before us, we naturally assume that Peter here refers to 1 Peter; and this may indeed be the case.[37] But Peter probably wrote more letters than have been included in the canon. Paul, for instance, mentions at least three letters that we do not have: a letter previous to 1 Corinthians (1 Cor. 5:9); a "severe" letter to the Corinthians, written between 1 and 2 Corinthians (2 Cor. 7:8); and a letter to the Laodiceans (Col. 4:16). Peter may, then, be referring to a letter we do not possess.[38]

Wholesome thinking (3:1). "Thinking" translates a noun (*dianoia*) that occurred frequently in certain philosophical circles in ancient Greece; indeed, the exact phrase Peter uses here (*eilikrinē dianoia*) occurs in Plato, though Peter does not use the phrase with the same philosophical associations. Rather, he does here what he has so skillfully done throughout the letter: utilize words and phrases from Greco-Roman philosophy and religion to

REFLECTIONS

AT KEY JUNCTURES IN THIS LETTER, Peter repeatedly calls on his readers to remember or recall the truth of Christ (1:12–13; 3:2; cf. the negative "forget" in 3:5, 8). He wants us not simply to call to mind some facts we may have forgotten but to dwell on biblical truth in such a way that it transforms our thinking and behavior. We may have a solid mental understanding of the "facts" of the faith: that Christ died for me, that he was raised, that I am indwelt by the Holy Spirit, and so on. But do we allow these truths to penetrate our minds and take possession of us? God called on his Old Testament people to "remember" their deliverance from Egypt so that they would always appreciate God's gracious work in their history (Ex. 13:3, 9; Deut. 7:18). Believers need to reflect similarly on the gracious work of God in Christ on our behalf.

communicate Christian truth to an audience apparently familiar with such language.

The words spoken in the past by the holy prophets (3:2). The reference (as in the somewhat parallel 1:20) is to the Old Testament prophets, who predicted that God would bring his plan to its climax through an earth-shaking event at the end of history.

The command given by our Lord and Savior through your apostles (3:2). The singular "command" gathers up the various elements of New Testament ethical teaching into one overall category. The false teachers, as we have seen, combined eschatological skepticism with ethical unconcern. Peter, by contrast, insists that his readers be mindful of the teaching of Jesus about true discipleship—a teaching passed on to them through the apostles.

In the last days scoffers will come (3:3). The future tense has the same explanation as the one in 2:1: Peter cites earlier predictions about what is, in fact, taking place in his own time. The early Christians believed that, with the coming of Messiah and pouring out of the Spirit, the "last days" predicted by the prophets had arrived (see, e.g., Acts 2:17–18; Heb. 1:2). Thus, they could apply predictions about those days to their own situations. Peter may particularly have in mind Matthew 24:5: "Many will come in my name, claiming, 'I am the Christ,' and will deceive many." Note Paul's similar predictions:

> I know that after I leave, savage wolves will come in among you and will not spare the flock. Even from your own number men will arise and distort the truth in order to draw away disciples after them. (Acts 20:29–30)

> The Spirit clearly says that in later times some will abandon the truth and follow deceiving spirits and things taught by demons. (1 Tim. 4:1)

However, while the "last days" will be especially marked by "scoffers," the phenomenon is nothing new in the history of God's people. The psalmist pronounced "blessed" the person who does not "sit in the seat of the mockers" (Ps. 1:1). Likewise, Proverbs cautions the righteous to avoid the ways of the "mocker" (Prov. 1:22; 9:7–8; 13:1).

They will say, "Where is this 'coming' he promised?" (3:4). The form of the question reminds us of some Old Testament passages where sinners express their unbelief or mockery. For example:

> You have wearied the LORD with your words. "How have we wearied him?" you ask. By saying, "All who do evil are good in the eyes of the LORD, and he is pleased with them" or "Where is the God of justice?" (Mal. 2:17)

> They keep saying to me, "Where is the word of the LORD? Let it now be fulfilled!" (Jer. 17:15)

Our fathers (3:4). Some scholars seize on this reference as clear evidence that Peter could not have written this letter. The "fathers," they argue, must be the first generation of Christian believers, since the whole issue in the context is about the reality of Christ's returning in glory. But the evidence is by no means clear. There is no "our" in the Greek text, so Peter simply refers to "the fathers."

This word occurs elsewhere in the New Testament as a reference to the patriarchs (cf. Rom. 9:5; 11:28; 15:8). Moreover, as we have seen ("prophets" in 2 Peter 3:2), Peter is concerned to ground the fact of a climactic judgment at the end of history in the teaching of the Old Testament (cf. also the reference to the flood in 3:6).

Died (3:4). The Greek here is actually "fallen asleep" (*ekoimēthēsan*). Some scholars insist that this word is used for death in the New Testament as a reflection of the special Christian perspective on death. "Sleep" connotes the truth that believers are to be raised from their dead state to live again (cf. esp. John 11:11). But the Greeks had used the language of "sleep " to describe death since the time of Homer; note the way the Roman writer Catullus puts it: "The sun can set and rise again, but once our brief light sets, there is one unending night to be slept through" (5.4–6).

By God's word the heavens existed and the earth was formed out of water and by water (3:5). A better translation, recognizing the typical biblical idiom of "heavens and earth," is the REB: "There were heavens and earth long ago, created by God's word out of water and with water." The instrumentality of God's word in creation is, of course, clear enough, attested in many Old Testament texts. In addition to the creation account itself, see, for instance, Psalm 33:6: "By the word of the LORD were the heavens made."

But why does Peter mention "water" as a second instrument of creation? This probably refers to the creation account, where water plays a prominent role. In Genesis 1:2, before God began to organize his creation, we read about the Spirit "hovering over the waters." These waters, which are apparently covering the entire globe, are separated as God makes the "sky" (Gk. *ouranos*, "heaven"; Gen. 1:6–8). Then God forms the dry land by gathering the water together (Gen. 1:9). Peter also introduces "water" here for rhetorical reasons, for he goes on to compare God's creation with his judging of the world through water (2 Peter 3:6).

The world of that time was deluged and destroyed (3:6). Does Peter's remark have any bearing on the vexing debate about the extent of the flood? Jewish sources certainly imply a destruction of the whole physical universe. See, for example, *1 Enoch* 83:3–5:

> I saw in a vision the sky being hurled down and snatched and falling upon the earth. When it fell upon the earth, I saw the earth being swallowed up into the great abyss, the mountains being suspended upon mountains, the hills sinking down upon the hills, and tall trees being uprooted and thrown and sinking into the great abyss. Thereupon a word fell from my mouth; and I began crying aloud, saying, "The earth is being destroyed."[39]

Nevertheless, Peter's shift from "heavens and earth" to a word that often refers to humankind (*kosmos*; NIV "world") might imply a focus on the destruction of people.

The present heavens and earth are reserved for fire (3:7). Only here in the Bible do we find a prediction of the eventual destruction of the universe through fire. The Stoics, an influential school of philosophers in Peter's day, taught just such an end of the universe; and some scholars think that Peter derives his teaching from this background. But the

Jewish Tradition Regarding God's Delay of His Judgment

Jews in the apocalyptic tradition theorized that God was delaying his judgment to give opportunity for people to repent. See, for example, *1 Enoch* 60:4–6:

> And Michael sent another angel from among the holy ones and he raised me up. And when he had raised me up, my spirit returned; for (I had fainted) because I could not withstand the sight of these forces and (because) heaven has stirred up and agitated itself. Then Michael said unto me, "What have you seen that has so disturbed you? This day of mercy has lasted until today; and he has been merciful and long-suffering toward those that dwell upon the earth. And when this day arrives—and the power, the punishment, and the judgment, which the Lord of the Spirits has prepared for those who do not worship the righteous judgment, for those who deny the righteous judgment, and for those who take his name in vain—it will become a day of covenant for the elect and inquisition for the sinners."

Peter essentially endorses this tradition, which had Old Testament roots.[A-2]

Old Testament often uses "fire" as an image of God's judgment. "See, the LORD is coming with fire, and his chariots are like a whirlwind; he will bring down his anger with fury, and his rebuke with flames of fire. For with fire and with his sword the LORD will execute judgment upon all men, and many will be those slain by the LORD."[40]

Living in Light of the End (3:8–13)

In contrast to the false teachers, who forget or deliberately suppress the truth about the end of the world, believers must not forget that this universe is not permanent, for God has appointed a day when he will judge it and usher in "a new heaven and a new earth." Peter urges his readers to live holy lives in light of this truth.

With the Lord one day is like a thousand years, and a thousand years are like a day (3:8). Peter adopts these words from Psalm 90:4: "For a thousand years in your sight are like a day that has just gone by, or like a watch in the night." God, being eternal, does not experience time as we do. Later Christians built elaborate systems of historical predictions on the basis of this text. They understood Psalm 90:4 as teaching that a biblical "day" would last a thousand years. They furthermore believed that the seven "days" of creation would be matched by seven "days" of world history. The seventh, the day of "rest," would be the Messianic age.[41] Peter betrays no evidence of any such application of the verse.

The Lord is not slow in keeping his promise (3:9). As we pointed out in the introduction, the false teachers may have been influenced by a certain skepticism about judgment that was widespread in the Greco-Roman world of that time. As Plutarch comments, "God's slowness [to judge] undermines our belief in providence."[42] At a later date, we find a rabbi uttering this curse: "Cursed be the bones of those who calculate the end. For they would say, since the predetermined time has arrived, and yet he has not come, he will never come" (*b. Sanh.* 97b).

He is patient with you, not wanting anyone to perish, but everyone to come to repentance (3:9). Theologians debate the significance of this text, questioning why anyone should ever be finally damned if, indeed, God "wills" no one to perish. But our concern must be with the possible background of this assertion. In this respect, we must refer to a widespread Jewish teaching directed to the problem of delay: Why was God waiting so long to vindicate his name and rescue his people from their trials? The answer took its lead from Habakkuk 2:3: "For the revelation awaits an appointed time; it speaks of the end and will not prove false. Though it linger, wait for it; it will certainly come and will not delay." Peter's comments are essentially in accord with Jewish apocalyptic tradition, which viewed God as delaying his judgment as a means of mercifully providing people with time to repent (see "Jewish Tradition Regarding God's Delay of His Judgment").

The elements will be destroyed by fire (3:10). "Elements" translates the Greek word *stoicheia*. Scholars debate its precise reference, especially in the Pauline phrase "the basic principles of the world" (Gal. 4:3; Col. 2:8, 20). Some think Paul refers to spiritual beings. But Peter cannot mean that, since this meaning is unattested in the New Testament outside Paul. Two alternatives are therefore left: the heavenly bodies, or the basic "building blocks" of the world. The former has in its favor the many Old Testament texts that predict a destruction of the heavenly bodies at the time of the judgment. Note, for instance, Isaiah 34:4: "All the stars of the heavens will be dissolved and the sky rolled up like a scroll; all the starry host will fall like withered leaves from the vine, like shriveled figs from the fig tree." But Peter's focus on the "earth" in this context favors the latter interpretation.

Everything in it will be laid bare (3:10). "Laid bare" translates a difficult word. Many manuscripts have the Greek word *katakaēsetai*, which can be rendered "burned up," an idea that would make perfect sense in a context in which Peter has already claimed that the earth is "reserved for fire" (3:7; cf. NASB). But it is just because this word fits so well that we should be suspicious of it on text-critical grounds. For the early scribes tended to substitute natural readings for what seemed to them more difficult ones. So we should probably accept the Greek word *heurethēsetai*, which means, literally, "will be found." This word can have the connotation "be manifest," with the nuance "before God"; this is the general idea that the NIV has adopted. On the Judgment Day all things will be manifest before God, "laid bare" to his scrutinizing assessment.

As you look forward to the day of God and speed its coming (3:12). How can believers "hasten" the coming of the day of God? Peter's words can be explained by recognizing his dependence on a widespread Jewish teaching to the effect that the repentance of God's people would bring in the final day. This tradition is well attested in a rabbinic text that purports to give a debate between two first-century rabbis. R. Joshua b. Hananiah argued that God had sovereignly determined the time of the end and that nothing could alter that decision. But R. Eliezer b. Hyrcanus maintained that Israel's repentance would trigger the events of the end (*b. Sanh.* 97–98). Peter himself seems to reflect the view of R. Eliezer in his speech in the temple precincts: "Repent, then, and turn to God, so that your sins may be wiped out, that times of refreshing may come from the Lord, and that he may send the Christ, who has been appointed for you—even Jesus" (Acts 3:19–20).

The elements will melt in the heat (3:12). The word "melt" (*tēkō*) is particularly appropriate in this context, since the Old Testament uses the same language to depict the cosmic disasters that accompany the Day of the Lord. See Micah 1:3–4: "Look! The LORD is coming from his dwelling place; he comes down and treads the high places of the earth. The mountains melt beneath him and the valleys split apart, like wax before the fire, like water rushing down a slope" (see also Isa. 63:19–64:1).

A new heaven and a new earth (3:13). The promise of a re-creation of the universe rests especially on Isaiah 65–66, the only Old Testament passage to speak about a "new heaven and new earth." See, for example, 65:17: "Behold, I will create new heavens and a new earth. The former things will not be remembered, nor will they come to mind" (cf. also 66:22; Rev. 21:1).

Concluding Exhortation (3:14–18)

Peter ends his letter on the note with which he began: an exhortation to believers to "grow in the grace and knowledge of our Lord and Savior Jesus Christ" (3:18; cf. 1:3–4). He underscores this exhortation with a reminder of the Lord's patience (3:14–16) and warns for a last time about the dangerous influence of the false teachers (3:17).

Make every effort to be found spotless (3:14). Peter echoes his command in 1:5 to "make every effort to add to your faith goodness" and the language of judicial scrutiny from 3:10. "To be found spotless" is to appear before God, the Judge, as righteous by virtue of Christ's work on our behalf on the last day.

Our dear brother Paul (3:15). Many believers have concluded from texts such as Galatians 2 that Paul and Peter were constantly at odds in the early church; an influential school of scholarship still assumes basically the same thing. But the New Testament generally portrays Peter and Paul as agreeing over the gospel and other key theological issues.[43] In addition, Silvanus, the scribe of 1 Peter, was a member of Paul's circle too.[44]

In all his letters (3:16). This need not mean that Peter was familiar with all the letters we now have in the New Testament. All Peter notes is that he has read some of Paul's letters and he finds them to focus on the same kind of matters Peter is writing about. We have no way to know what letters they may have been.

Hard to understand (3:16). The flavor of the Greek word here (*dysnoētos*) may be gauged from its application to Greek oracles. These oracles were often completely ambiguous, the most famous being the response of the Delphi oracle to a king asking if he should go to war: "If you go to war, you will destroy a great nation."[45] Whether the nation was his own or the one against which he fought was not clear.

The other Scriptures (3:16). The word *graphai* as used here and everywhere else in the New Testament refers to canonical books of the Old Testament. Peter therefore implicitly places the letters of Paul in the category of "biblical books"—an important early indication of the way some New Testament letters were being viewed. Somewhat similar is Paul's citation of a saying of Jesus as "Scripture" in 1 Timothy 5:18.

ANNOTATED BIBLIOGRAPHY

Bauckham, Richard. *Jude, 2 Peter*. WBC. Waco, Tex.: Word, 1983.

The most important conservative commentary on these letters in decades; arguably the best technical commentary now available. Rich in references to extrabiblical materials and marred only by its assumption of pseudonymity for 2 Peter.

Bigg, Charles. *A Critical and Exegetical Commentary on the Epistles of St. Peter and St. Jude*. ICC. New York: Scribners, 1903.

Classic treatment, oriented to historical and grammatical issues.

Kelly, J. N. D. *A Commentary on the Epistles of Peter and of Jude*. HNTC. New York: Harper & Row, 1969.

Careful treatment of the text.

Mayor, Joseph B. *The Epistle of St. Jude and the Second Epistle of St. Peter: Greek Text with Introduction, Notes and Comments*. Grand Rapids: Baker, 1979 (= 1907).

Lengthy treatment, focusing especially on historical and linguistic matters.

Moo, Douglas J. *2 Peter and Jude*. NIVAC. Grand Rapids: Zondervan, 1996.

Exposition of the English text with focus on contemporary application.

Neyrey, Jerome H. *2 Peter, Jude: A New Translation with Introduction and Commentary*. AB. Garden City, N.Y.: Doubleday, 1993.

The most recent English language technical commentary, incorporating social-critical and literary approaches.

CHAPTER NOTES

Main Text Notes

1. See, for instance, Donald Guthrie, *New Testament Introduction* (Downers Grove: InterVarsity, 1990), 805–42.
2. Eusebius, *HE* 2.25.8 .
3. *1 Clement* 5–6; Tacitus, *Ann.* 15.44.
4. See R. P. Martin, "Peter," in *ISBE*, 3.802–7.
5. See, e.g., J. N. D. Kelly, *A Commentary on the Epistles of Peter and of Jude* (HNTC; San Francisco: Harper & Row, 1969), 227–31.
6. See Jerome Neyrey, *2 Peter, Jude* (AB; New York: Doubleday, 1993), 123–24.
7. See esp. R. Bauckham, *2 Peter, Jude* (WBC; Waco, Tex.: Word, 1983), 131–35.
8. See further in D. E. Aune, "Religions, Greco-Roman," *DPL*, 792–93.
9. Philo, *Alleg. Interp.* 1.38.
10. See also Hermas, *Mandates* 5.2.4; *Visions* 3.8.7; *m. Sotah* 9:5. New Testament examples are found in Rom. 5:3–4 and James 1:2–4.
11. Aristotle, *Nicomachean Ethics* 7.1–11; Philo, *Spec. Laws* 2.195. See W. Grundmann, "ἐγράτεια," *TDNT*, 2.339–42, for additional references and discussion.
12. See, e.g., Philo, *Creation* 1; Josephus, *Ant.* 1.22.
13. Aristotle, *Metaphysics* 11.8.
14. Josephus, *Ant.* 3.5.2 §80.
15. Bauckham, *Jude, 2 Peter,* 221.
16. See also Isa. 11:11; 13:6, 9; 22:5; 34:8; Jer. 46:10; Ezek. 7:10; 13:5; 30:3; Joel 2:1–11; Amos 5:18–20; Zeph. 1:7–8, 14–18; Zech. 14:1.
17. Epiphanius, *Pamarion* 30.1.5.
18. Matt. 24:4–5, 10–11, 23–24.
19. Luke 2:29; Acts 4:24; Jude 4; Rev. 6:10.
20. Acts 5:17; 15:5; 24:5, 14; 26:5; 28:22; 1 Cor. 11:19; Gal. 5:20.
21. See, e.g., J. Calvin, *The Epistle of Paul the Apostle to the Hebrews and First and Second Epis-*

tles of St. Peter (reprint; Grand Rapids: Eerdmans, 1963), 348.
22. See also *Jub.* 5:1; 10:1–6; Josephus, *Ant.* 1.73; Philo, *Giants* 6; QG 1.92; CD 2:18.
23. See *1 En.* 20:2; *Sib. Or.* 4.186; Philo, *Moses* 2.433; *Rewards and Punishments* 152.
24. See, for example, Josephus, *Ant.* 1.3.1 §74; *Sib. Or.* 1.148–98, esp. 1.129.
25. Cf. also 1QH 10:8; *Ascen. Isa.* 9:32.
26. See, e.g., the LXX rendering of Ex. 15:11; Philo, *Spec. Laws* 1.45; *T. Judah* 25.2.
27. E.g., Juvenal 1.141; Pliny, *Natural History* 8.81.
28. Eccl. 10:16; Isa. 5:11; *T. Mos.* 7:4; Juvenal 1.103.
29. See G. Wainwright, "Lord's Supper, Love Feast," *DLNT*, 686–94.
30. Cf. Plutarch, *Moralia* 528E.
31. 1 Sam. 12:23; Ps. 107:7; Prov. 2:13; Isa. 33:15; Acts 9:2; 19:9, 23; 22:4; 24:14, 22.
32. See also Josh. 13:22; 24:9–10; Neh. 13:1–2; Mic. 6:5; Jude 11; Rev. 2:14.
33. See, e.g., Philo, *Moses* 1.266–68.
34. Philo, *Moses* 2.193.
35. Aristotle, *Meteor.* 1.346B.
36. See Bauckham, *Jude, 2 Peter,* 279.
37. Most commentators agree; see, e.g., C. Bigg, *A Critical and Exegetical Commentary on the Epistles of St. Peter and St. Jude* (ICC; New York: Scribners, 1903), 288–89.
38. See, e.g., E. M. B. Green, *The Second Epistle General of Peter and the General Epistle of Jude* (TNTC; Grand Rapids: Eerdmans, 1968), 123–24.
39. See also Philo, *Moses* 2.63–65.
40. Isa. 66:15–16; cf. also 30:30; Nah. 1:6; Zeph. 1:18; 3:8.
41. See, e.g., Justin, *Dialogue* 81; *Barn.* 15.4.
42. Plutarch, *Moralia* 549b.
43. See, e.g., Acts 11:2–18; 15:7–11.
44. See 1 Peter 5:12; cf. Acts 15:40; 1 Thess. 1:1.
45. Aristotle, *Rhetoric* 3.5.

Sidebar and Chart Notes

A-1. See the survey in M. J. Harris, *From Grave to Glory: Resurrection in the New Testament* (Grand Rapids: Zondervan, 1990), 36–40.
A-2. See also Wisd. Sol. 11:23; *4 Ezra* 3:30; 7:33, 134; *2 Apoc. Bar.* 89:12.; Joel 2:12–13.

I JOHN

by Robert Yarbrough

The Setting of 1 John

First John was apparently quoted as early as the end of the first century A.D. by Papias of Hierapolis, whose writings we may place at about A.D. 95–110.[1] Polycarp's letter to the Philippians (early second century) likewise shows knowledge of 1 John (*Phil.* 7:1). John's first letter is one of the best attested letters in the New Testament.

Now both Papias and Polycarp of Smyrna were residents of western Asia Minor, not far from the major cultural center of Ephesus. This may be the reason they knew John's letter, for late in life John was a spiritual leader in that part of the Mediterranean world. He apparently lived in Ephesus and helped administer church affairs in the surrounding region.[2] He lived to a great old age and was still active at the beginning of the reign of the Roman emperor Trajan (A.D. 98–117).

This is probably the best tangible clue to the geographical setting of this letter. Although 1 John lacks explicit reference to city or region, it

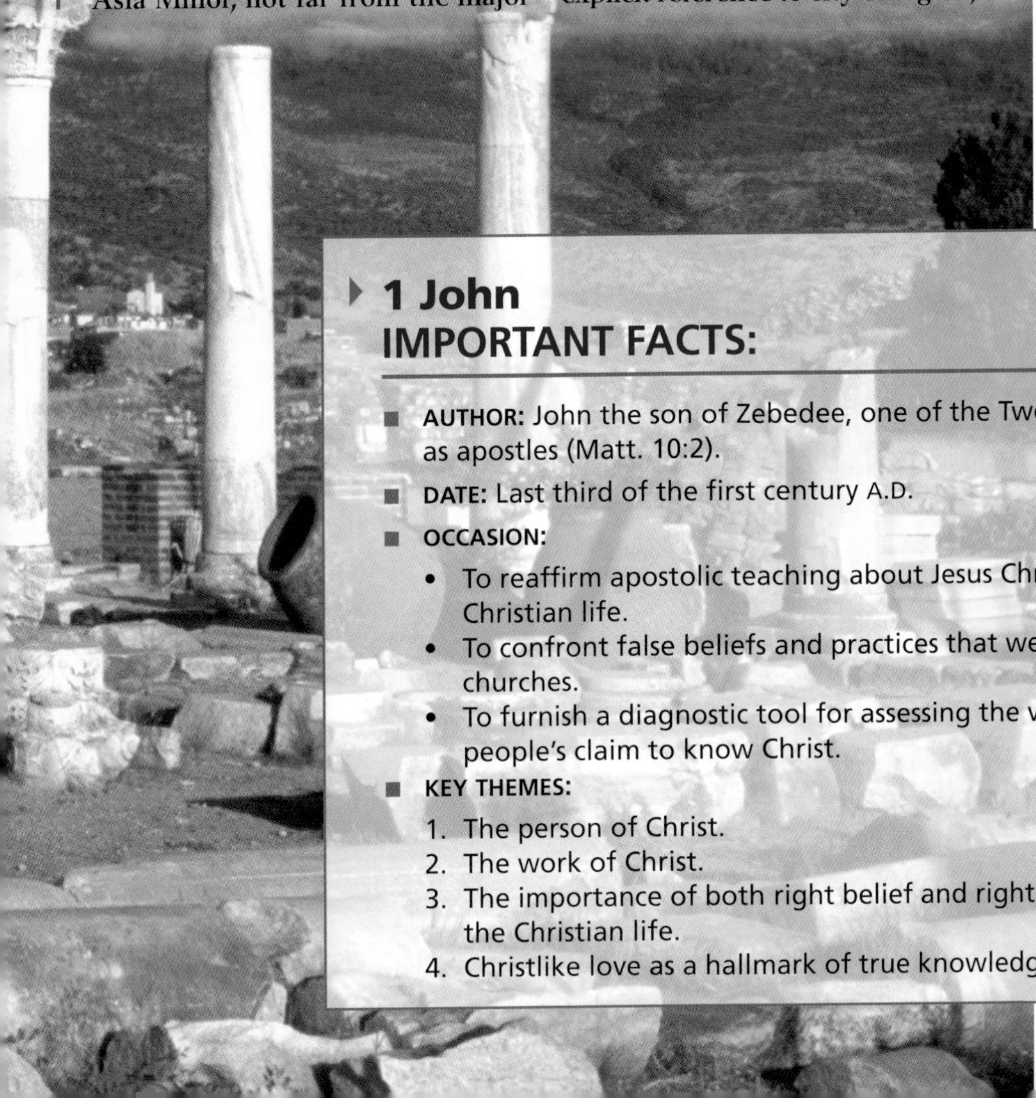

REMAINS OF THE FOURTH-CENTURY A.D. CHURCH OF ST. JOHN NEAR EPHESUS

1 John IMPORTANT FACTS:

- **AUTHOR:** John the son of Zebedee, one of the Twelve chosen as apostles (Matt. 10:2).
- **DATE:** Last third of the first century A.D.
- **OCCASION:**
  - To reaffirm apostolic teaching about Jesus Christ and the Christian life.
  - To confront false beliefs and practices that were harming churches.
  - To furnish a diagnostic tool for assessing the validity of people's claim to know Christ.
- **KEY THEMES:**
  1. The person of Christ.
  2. The work of Christ.
  3. The importance of both right belief and right practice in the Christian life.
  4. Christlike love as a hallmark of true knowledge of God.

is most likely that John is speaking to problems that have arisen in the churches over which he has some jurisdiction. These may well include those congregations to whom he addressed part of the book of Revelation—Ephesus, Smyrna, Pergamum, Thyatira, Sardis, Philadelphia, and Laodicea (Rev. 2–3).[3]

Problems in the Churches

Since 1 John is not addressed to any specific leader or location, we can assume it was meant for a group of churches facing similar challenges. If their general location was the Roman province of Asia, we are on firmest historical ground if we infer first of all from Revelation (which addresses churches in Asian cities) features of local belief or practice known to be at work in the churches that might well have created confusion about the gospel.

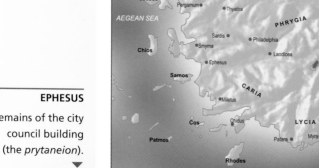

WESTERN ASIA MINOR

EPHESUS

Remains of the city council building (the *prytaneion*).

Influence of false teachers. First John (e.g., 2:18–19; 4:6) addresses a cultural setting in which key leaders are seeking to lead churches in a direction different from that laid out by Jesus Christ through hand-picked disciples like John. At Ephesus there are "wicked men . . . who claim to be apostles but are not" (Rev. 2:2). Among these are the Nicolaitans (2:6), a group that apparently rose within the church and promoted pagan sexual morals. They are also making their presence felt at Smyrna (2:15). At Thyatira a similar crisis has arisen. A woman whom John calls Jezebel[4] claims to have prophetic gifts. She teaches people "deep secrets" of Satan (2:24). Like the Nicolaitans she lures followers toward immoral sexual expression (2:20). This seems to have been a widespread problem in certain segments of the early church (2 Peter 2:15; Jude 11).

Influence of lax practice. From earliest times the God of the Bible called for a faith that expressed itself in loving obedience (Deut. 6:4ff.). Jesus, Paul, and other New Testament writers (e.g., James) preached a faith that was to be rich in works.[5] First John addresses readers who seem to have lost sight of the active nature of biblical faith.[6] This is known to have become a problem at Ephesus, where the church has forsaken its "first love" and has to be told, "Repent and do the things you did at first" (Rev. 2:5). At Thyatira and Philadelphia believers are told to "hold on" to what they have until Christ comes (2:25; 3:11).

More gravely, Christ warns the church at Sardis: "I have not found your deeds complete in the sight of my God" (3:2). There are only "a few people" there "who have not soiled their clothes," that is, not fallen prey to sub-Christian behavior patterns. Laodicea's level of active commitment is revoltingly tepid in Christ's sight (3:16). If these historic churches are in any way similar to the situation 1 John addresses, then the letter's numerous references to lax practice make good sense.

Influence of hostile rival religions and the threat of persecution. Whatever the situation of the churches that receive 1 John, it is not a religious vacuum. John has to encourage readers to stand their ground and not be intimidated by forces arrayed against them (e.g., 4:4–5). Religious leaders (see above) hostile to gospel belief and practice preside over quasi-Christian splinter groups or non-Christian currents that defy and even persecute the fledgling apostolic churches.

The Nicolaitans have already been mentioned. At Smyrna are self-proclaimed Jews on the verge of imprisoning Christians and even hastening their deaths (Rev. 2:9–10). At Philadelphia is a "synagogue of Satan," whom Christ promises to bring to its knees in recognition of his presence among the true people of God (3:9). Rival groups at Pergamum teach idolatrous and immoral doctrines that appear to have been worked out in practice (2:14). Christ warns that he will strike dead those pseudo-Christians at Thyatira who have been seduced by the Jezebel movement (2:23). At Sardis the majority of the visible church is charged with having "a reputation of being alive, but you are dead" (3:1). Things are no better at Laodicea, a church denounced by Christ as lukewarm and so blind that it cannot see its own poverty (3:17–18). First John likely addresses a situation where aberrant religious views and even persecution threaten to jeopardize the integrity of many churches in God's sight.

Challenges Confronting the Churches

The problems cropping up in churches have points of contact, if not their origin, on the outside. There are numerous possibilities here but few sure facts. If 1 John is written as late as the A.D. 90s, then one

EPHESUS

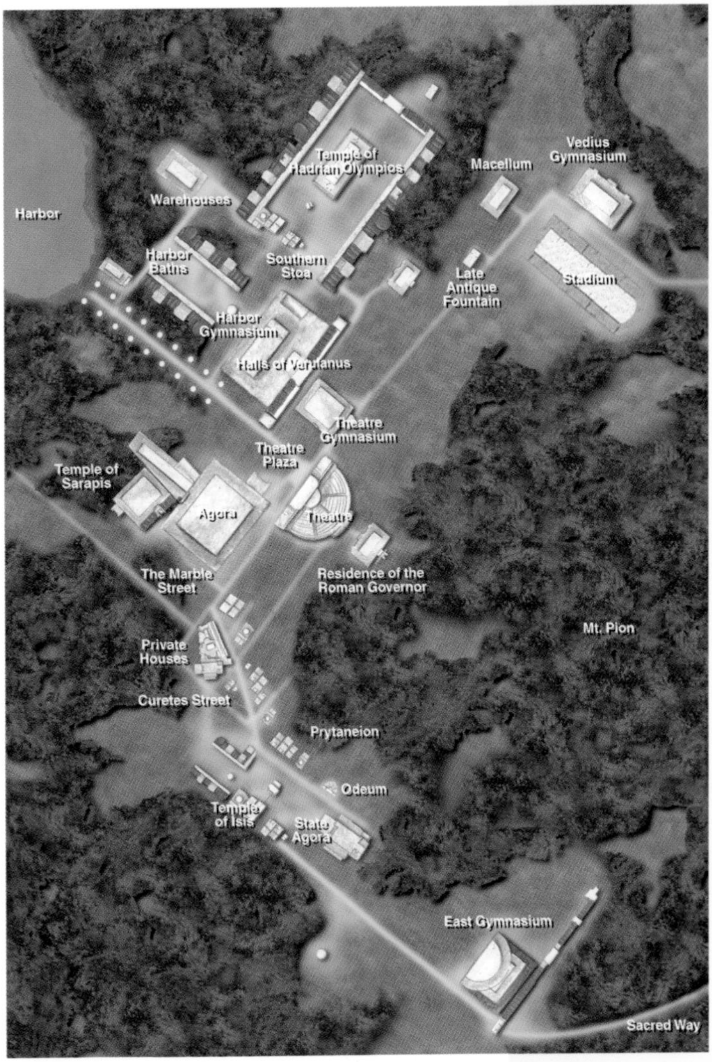

Imperial Persecution of Christians

While some later Christian writers may overdramatize Roman persecution of Christians in the first century, there is no doubt that the extent of it was serious. A well-known modern scholar of early church history comments on Domitian, the emperor said to have banished the apostle John to Patmos and to have persecuted many other Christians as well:

> The effect of Domitian's measures ... was to increase the legal distinctions between Jews and Christians in the eyes of the authorities to the disadvantage of the Christians, for these were now deprived of their one claim to legality. Domitian was not the man to tolerate religious deviations. When one discounts the senatorial prejudices of Tacitus and Suetonius [Roman historians who wrote critically of Domitian], the Emperor stands out as a shrewd but jealous-minded ruler, a strong upholder of public right and the state religion, whose prejudices and fears for his own safety increased with age.[A-1]

challenge to faith may be imperial persecution. The emperor Domitian (ruled A.D. 81–96) is thought to have made things hard for a number of groups, including Christians (see "Imperial Persecution of Christians," below).[7]

EPHESIAN INSCRIPTION

The monument was erected in honor of Gaius Laicanius Bassus, the Roman proconsul (A.D. 80–81).

A second challenge may have been the first phase of the later well-known movement called Gnosticism. The views of groups known by this name are varied, and they never formed a unified body of faith and practice in the same way that the apostolic churches did. But as a whole, and in confusingly varied ways, they taught that salvation was by esoteric knowledge, not by Christ's atoning death and bodily resurrection. For gnostics, created matter (including the human body, and therefore even Jesus' body) was inherently evil, so salvation involved a flight from bodily existence, not resurrection of the body to eternal life. This flight sometimes resulted in asceticism, harsh treatment of the body—as if punishing it would demonstrate that the flesh was nothing. In other cases the gnostics' low view of the body resulted in moral license—if the body is nothing, why not indulge it as a means of expressing the irrelevance of bodily deeds and the transcendence of the redeemed spirit over fleshly constraints?

Gnostic views of Christ varied. Some were docetic, believing that Christ was divine but did not really become fully human (cf. 4:2). A group following a leader called Cerinthus (see "Irenaeus and Cerinthus") taught that a divine spirit came on Jesus, making him divine in a sense—while denying Jesus' full and essential deity. "Jesus" and "Christ" were ultimately two different beings (see John's response in 2:22).

We cannot be sure that John addresses the problem of Gnosticism in its technical sense, which dates to the time after he wrote. But even if he does not, there are features of religious thought and practice that his first letter seeks to correct that later came to be associated with Gnostic religion.

The errors that 1 John decries may also have points of contact with more generic pagan or Jewish belief. The commentary below will explore these possibilities at the appropriate junctures.

Structure of the Letter

Numerous outlines of 1 John have been proposed. None has won universal agreement.[8] John seems to proceed in a topical rather than logical fashion. He "has no intention of producing a systematic treatment like that of Romans or Galatians."[9] He mentions a topic, elaborates on it, then drops it and goes to another, only to return to the first one at some later point. Some topics he touches on repeatedly; others he mentions but once or twice. The power of his counsel lies in its concentrated focus and cumulative effect, not its logically compelling systematic development.

In comments below we follow the paragraph divisions used by ancient Greek copyists.[10] They divided the letter into seven sections (see chart "Structure of 1 John"). The chart's divisions are more rhetorical than material in nature. They have the advantage of not imposing a material structure on a letter that tends to proceed by digressions rather than by closely reasoned sequential units.

Gospel Foundations: Beginnings and True Light (1:1–2:6)

John writes not as an academic theorist but as a pastoral leader troubled by error

▸ Irenaeus on Cerinthus

The second-century Christian leader Irenaeus wrote extensively about religious movements that mixed Christian language with unchristian convictions and practices. A leader of one of these movements, very likely gnostic in nature, was Cerinthus:

Cerinthus, again, a man who was educated in the wisdom of the Egyptians, taught that the world was not made by the primary God, but by a certain Power far separated from him, and at a distance from that Principality who is supreme over the universe, and ignorant of him who is above all. He represented Jesus as having not been born of a virgin, but as being the son of Joseph and Mary according to the ordinary course of human generation, while he was nevertheless more righteous, prudent, and wise than other men. Moreover, after his baptism, Christ descended upon him in the form of a dove from the Supreme Ruler, and that then he proclaimed the unknown Father, and performed miracles. But at last Christ departed from Jesus, and that then Jesus suffered and rose again, while Christ remained impassible [unaffected by suffering or feeling], inasmuch as he was a spiritual being.[A-2]

Structure of 1 John		
Opening Words	**Verses**	**Statement of**
"That which was from the beginning . . ."	1:1–2:6	Central burden: God is light
"My dear children . . ."	2:7–17	Central command: Heed the age-old message
"Dear children . . ."	2:18–3:8	Key counsel: Remain in his anointing and receive eternal life
"No one who is born of God will continue to sin . . ."	3:9–4:6	Central warning: Beware Cain's error and false prophets
"Dear friends . . ."	4:7–14	Foundational assurance: God's love
"If anyone acknowledges that Jesus is the Son of God . . ."	4:15–5:15	Necessary instruction: Believing in Jesus the Christ, the Son of God
"If anyone sees a brother commit a sin . . ."	5:16–21	Concluding admonition: The true God and the threat of impostors

and discord in Christ's churches. In this first section of his letter he touches on a number of key concerns: the genuineness of the Christian message, the validity of the apostles' witness, the nature of God, the weightiness of sin, the goals of his letter, the atoning ministry of Jesus Christ, the effect of God's love, and more. All of these relate to what John sees as original and therefore foundational because they relate to "that which was from the beginning"—Jesus Christ.

Having established these claims and concerns in the letter's opening lines, he will return to them repeatedly in subsequent sections.

"IN THE BEGINNING. . ."

From the beginning (1:1). In the modern West, newest is best—new ideas, new cars, new beliefs. But in John's world, for something to be true it must be shown to have an ancient heritage. This conviction lies behind the Gospel genealogies (Matt. 1; Luke 3). Jesus assumes it in his disputes with opponents: He is more ancient than their ancestor Abraham (John 8:58). Eusebius (ca. A.D. 300) commends his *Ecclesiastical History* because by it "the real antiquity and divine character of Christianity will be . . . demonstrated to those who suppose that it is recent and foreign, appearing no earlier than yesterday."[11] Even Moses, as he compiled Genesis, realized the importance of showing that his account connects with the world's primal beginnings (Gen. 1:1). As John addresses troubled churches, he grounds the basis for his remarks in the antiquity of what he has seen.

We (1:1). The "we" refers to the earliest disciples, especially the apostles—those who personally saw and lived with Jesus in his earthly days. Why are witnesses important? Jesus appointed the apostles to be his witnesses (Acts 1:8; cf. 1:2). He is in line here with Moses, who taught that testimony must be based on two or more witnesses (Deut. 19:15). This rule was observed in the early church (2 Cor. 13:1). It was likewise observed in Judaism, as reflected in the attempt to establish credible testimony at Jesus' trial (Matt. 26:60).[12] Like John, Luke claims that his Gospel is based on eyewitness testimony (Luke 1:2).

Heard . . . seen . . . looked at . . . touched (1:1). John's letter, he claims, is based on truth. That is, the things he will say about Jesus Christ correspond to the way Jesus actually appeared, lived, died, and rose. For John and others had heard, seen, and touched him. Ancient writers who spoke about historical matters—Jesus of Nazareth's coming *is* a historical and not just religious fact—were concerned that their reports be accurate.[13] Social stability was threatened when people no longer told the truth.[14] Those claiming to relate historical matters must adhere to the facts on which knowledge of history is based.[15] The historian Plutarch (ca. A.D. 100) distinguished between "conjecture" and "definite historical evidence" (*Fall of the Roman Republic, Gaius Marius* 11).[16] John had personal, extensive, and tangible proof—shared with others, so it could not be personal delusion—to back up his letter's teaching about Jesus.

Philo points out that some authorities in ancient times threw out evidence based on hearing alone, "on the ground that what is believed through the eyes is true but through hearing is false."[17] Seneca warns that "credulity is a source of very great mischief. . . . We should believe only what is thrust under our eyes and becomes unmistakable . . . and develop the habit of being slow to believe" (*On Anger* 2.24). Whether hearing, seeing, or touch is demanded for validation, John can vouch for the truth of what he claims (see comments on 1 John 5:9).

Eternal life (1:2). See comments on 2:25.

Fellowship . . . with the Father and with his Son (1:3). See comments on 1:7.

Joy (1:4). See comments on 2 John 4.

God is light (1:5). This, John says, is the core of his letter's message. By this he refers primarily to God's moral excellence,

REFLECTIONS

NORTH AMERICAN CHURCH PUBLICITY OFTEN MAKES use of the phrase "food, fun, and fellowship." But for John and his readers "fellowship" is apparently something more profound than good food and good times. Judging from John's letter, fellowship involves commitment to a common body of belief (doctrine) and faithfulness in a dedicated life of obedience. It also involves that elusive thing called love—love for God as well as love for people and especially fellow believers.

So where do "food" and "fun" fit in? In the early church the Lord's Supper was probably observed weekly and involved a full meal. Recreational eating was not the goal, but the shared table was part of corporate worship. As for fun, in a social setting where the very survival of the church was an ongoing challenge, just being able to celebrate another week of life in Christ and shared ministry as God's people might have seemed cause enough to rejoice.

his separateness from all darkness and evil. (On God's character, see "God's Moral Perfection," below. On God as light, see "The True Light" at 2:9.)

The connection between "God" and "light" has little to do with either gnostic or Qumran thought.[18] It is rather from the Old Testament, first of all, that John would have first gained associations between God and light. God made the light of the physical world (Gen. 1:3). He gave his people visual light during their escape from Egypt (Ex. 13:21). David extolled God's spiritual light in prayer (2 Sam. 22:29); with his last words he praised the divine radiance: God "is like the light of morning at sunrise on a cloudless morning" (2 Sam. 23:4). Micah proclaimed, "Though I have fallen, I will rise. Though I sit in darkness, the LORD will be my light" (Mic. 7:8). Like Micah John underscores God's moral light. He knows that in the church age, as at other times in redemptive history, there are "those who call evil good and good evil, who put darkness for light and light for darkness" (Isa. 5:20). They are morally blinded.

Not only God but also Jesus is "light" in John's writings (John 8:12; 9:5). Jesus said, "I have come into the world as a light, so that no one who believes in me should stay in darkness" (12:46).

John's "God is light" stands in contrast with pagan religious systems whose gods or goddesses were associated with the heavenly bodies. Under Roman rule the Syrian Baal, for example, was associated with the sun; his female consort was the moon.[19] Well after New Testament times a cult arose that worshiped the sun.[20] But the true God is personal, not a distant gleam in the night darkness, or even the blazing fire of sunlight. He gives light, ethical direction, rather than condoning harmful or lawless acts. He creates the natural light but is in no way to be identified with it. We can all see the sun, but no one has ever seen God (John 1:18).

At the core of John's letter is the conviction that there is a light, peculiar to God the Father though shared with Christ the Son, which those who know God recognize. Those who do not know God will not recognize that intimate Father-Son connection but will define one apart from the other. Much of 1 John addresses the evils that arise when this occurs.

ZEUS

Marble statue of the god from Istanbul.

The truth (1:6, 8; 2:4). See comments on 2 John 1.

The blood of Jesus . . . purifies us from all sin (1:7). If God is perfectly pure and people are weighed down by sin, how can they be brought together? How can there be "fellowship . . . with the Father and with his Son" (1:3)? John's answer: through Jesus' death on the cross—his blood shed for sin.

Others in John's day would have completely disagreed. Philo (influenced by Stoic doctrine) writes that "reason is a priest."[21] Thinking the right thoughts and

God's Moral Perfection in the Ancient World

John's claim that "God is light; in him there is no darkness at all" (1 John 1:5) expresses a widespread Jewish conviction grounded in many Old Testament passages. The Alexandrian Jewish writer Philo (ca. 20 B.C.–A.D. 50) writes most emphatically: "God is absolutely not the cause of any evil whatever of any kind."[A-3]

In traditional Greek religion, which was part of the seedbed of Gnosticism, the gods were not morally upright at all. Xenophanes (c. 570–488 B.C.) writes: "Both Homer and Hesiod have attributed to the gods all things that are shameful and a reproach among mankind: theft, adultery, and mutual deception."[A-4]

saying no to bodily pleasures will purify from sin: "The perfect man is always trying to attain to a complete emancipation from the power of the passions" (3.131). The notion of reason, or knowledge, being the key to salvation is foundational to Gnosticism. It is grounded in the older conviction of Greek religion that reason is the key to blessedness.

In contrast to this, John does not think the human mind can attain what is necessary for salvation. Only an act of God can provide this, and that act is the saving death of Jesus, which saves all who believe (John 1:12).

Without sin (1:8). Numerous Old Testament passages insist that everyone has sinned.[22] The Jewish writer Philo states, "To be aware of what one has done amiss, and to blame one's self, is the part of a righteous man."[23] Even more explicitly, he writes that "there is no man who self-sustained has run the course of life from birth to death without stumbling, but in every case his footsteps have slipped through errors, some voluntary, some involuntary."[24]

In pagan thinking clear moral standards were lacking. "In general the standard was public opinion and not a code of conduct."[25] But there was still an awareness of sin. For example, in the ancient Greek religion Orphism one could receive punishment for sins in the afterlife.[26] The Latin poet Horace (65–8 B.C.) decries the sins of individuals and society at some length.[27]

John writes to sharpen awareness that humans too easily digress from divine standards—and then deceive themselves into protesting their innocence (see "Philo on Sin and Self-Deception").

If anybody does sin (2:1). If sin is the problem, what is the solution? It is Jesus, "who speaks to the Father in our defense" (2:1). Other faith communities of John's day saw the matter differently. Jews at Qumran believed that no willful sin against Moses' law could be forgiven; even minor sins required lengthy periods of penance, and atonement for sin took place through human acts of prayer and complete obedience to the community's teaching.[28] Yet there was hope through God's mercy and pardon (11.11–15). But the basis for hope is frustratingly vague.

John's prescription for forgiveness is as definite as it is simple: "Jesus Christ, the Righteous One." Writing shortly after John's death, Ignatius warns the church at Smyrna against those who deny the atoning power (cf. 1 John 2:2) of Jesus' death: "Let no man be misled. Even the heavenly beings and the glory of the angels and the rulers, both visible and invisible, are also subject to judgment, if they do not believe in the blood of Christ."[29]

Atoning sacrifice (2:1). The Greek word is *hilasmos* (used also in 4:10), a word associated with the Hebrew *kpr* word group found extensively (112 times) in the Old Testament. In some contexts the word means "to remove or wipe away." But it can also refer to a death by one victim that satisfies the guilt before God of some other victim. That is, a *hilasmos* ("propitiation" or "propitiatory sacrifice") bears God's wrath toward sin so that the sinner who deserves wrath may escape. Paul describes this process in 2 Corinthians 5:21: "God made him who had no sin to be sin for us, so that in him we might become the righteousness of God." That is, "God presented him as a sacrifice of atonement" (*hilastērion*; Rom. 3:25). John's usage carries the same notion. In most world religions, people do things to make themselves acceptable to God. For John, Jesus' death is the basis for forgiveness and salvation, not human merit.

The sins of the whole world (2:2). While John does not believe everyone will go to heaven, he states that Christ's saving

right ▶

ADVOCATE

Statue of a Roman lawyer in a toga.

▶ Philo on Sin and Self-Deception

John feels the need to warn readers about taking sin lightly. Philo elaborates on the human tendency toward flagrant sin and forgetfulness of both personal error and morality itself:

Therefore men in general, even if the slightest breeze of prosperity blows their way for only a moment, become puffed up and give themselves great airs, becoming insolent to all those who are in a lower condition than themselves, and calling them dregs of the earth, and annoyances, and sources of trouble, and burdens of the earth, and all sorts of names of that kind, as if they had been thoroughly able to establish the undeviating character of their prosperity on a solid foundation, though, very likely, they will not remain in the same condition even till tomorrow, for there is nothing more inconstant than fortune, which tosses human affairs up and down like dice. Often has a single day thrown down the man who was previously placed on an eminence, and raised the lowly man on high. And while men see these events continually taking place, and though they are well assured of the fact, still they overlook their relations and friends, and transgress the laws according to which they were born and brought up . . . no longer remembering a single one of their ancient usages.[A-5] death has opened blessings to all persons. In keeping with the universal scope of Christ's blessing, not many years after John's death Ignatius writes to Christians in Asia Minor: "Pray continually for the rest of mankind as well, that they may find God, for there is in them a hope of repentance."[30] Many religions of antiquity were focused primarily on the people group that practiced them. The Christian gospel, rooted in the knowledge of the one true God who created heaven and earth, had a comprehensive saving scope.

God's love is truly made complete (2:5). John, probably writing from Ephesus, teaches that obeying God's Word is a mark of being perfected in God's love. Ignatius warns the Ephesian Christians against people who traffic in God's name but disobey his commands: "For there are some who maliciously and deceitfully are accustomed to carry about the Name while doing other things unworthy of God."[31] But he commends the Ephesians: "So you are all fellow pilgrims . . . adorned in every respect with the commandments of Jesus Christ."[32]

The fact is that for many religions of that time obedience to a moral standard was not important at all. Social morality was at a low ebb. Immoral sexual practice was widespread. Religion did little to check these trends. Sometimes it even encouraged them. "Cultus had little to do with morality except in cases of grave offence, and priests did not function as moral guides."[33] Part of the reason for this lay in the Greek belief that reason, not revelation, was the sole foundation for knowing how to live. Xenophanes (c. 570–488 B.C.) wrote: "Truly the gods have not revealed to mortals all things from the beginning, but mortals by long seeking discover what is better."[34]

In contrast, John announces what is "from the beginning" (1 John 1:1), a God who loves (see comments on 4:8) and who reveals his will in Scripture and then in human hearts. God's love is completed as his people "walk as Jesus did" (2:6).

◀ *left*

MERCY SEAT

A representation of the high priest sprinkling blood on the mercy seat (or atonement cover) in the Most Holy Place on the Day of Atonement.

Statement of the Letter's Central Command: Heed the Age-Old Message (2:7–17)

If the preceding section is a kaleidoscope of concerns and assertions, this section is a microscope focused on one issue: the imperative to love—and to direct love to the proper objects. This imperative is not some new message but has a distinguished pedigree. At the same time it is new indeed.

Not . . . a new command but an old one, which you have had since the beginning (2:7). By "command" in this section John most likely refers to the imperative to love. It is "old" in the sense that it goes back to Moses' time, as John would have learned from the synagogue as well as from Jesus. (It is even more ancient than Moses, of course, in that it is grounded in God's eternal character and existence.)

Jesus' teaching on love is not something he inaugurated but something he inherited from the Hebrew Scriptures: "All the Law and the Prophets hang on these two commandments," Jesus said (Matt. 22:37–40): "Love the LORD your God with all your heart and with all your soul and with all your strength" (Deut. 6:5); "love your neighbor as yourself" (Lev. 19:18). This twofold ancient command—for John grounds the love that people express in the love that God has revealed (1 John 4:10)—is the heart of the message Christians receive.

But old messages are easy to forget. The Old Testament reminds readers many times to remember God: "Remember the wonders he has done, his miracles, and the judgments he pronounced" (Ps. 105:5). And even when memory is active, response may be lacking. The Greek writer Xenophon (4th century B.C.) wrote that the very oldest laws of the Greeks were widely praised, but they were not heeded.[35] Nor did these laws center on love but on virtuous and gentlemanly character, in the thinking of the Spartan law-giver Lycurgus (9th century B.C.).[36]

Old messages may also be overlooked because they are out of step with the times. In the modern West a basic belief is "individualist realism."[37] In such an outlook "I" am the center of my life, not other people. Love for others becomes a secondary concern; self-love is primary. John does not share this cultural outlook because it is not the outlook endorsed by God and instilled by the Christian message. Rather, the age-old reality to which God's love calls us is love—for God and for others, especially brothers and sisters in the faith.

Yet I am writing you a new command (2:8). Often John writes in terms of black-white contrasts. But here he speaks not of "either-or" but of "both-and." The love command is very old, but it is also very new.

The command is new because Jesus reaffirmed and dramatized it in unprecedented ways. Jesus dramatized love by the way he experienced it from God:

The True Light

God, his ways, and his word are associated with light in numerous ancient writings. An example would be the *Odes of Solomon*, a poetic book perhaps composed in Syriac and dating from around A.D. 100:

> The Lord has directed my mouth by his Word,
> and has opened my heart by his Light. (10:1)
> And the Lord renewed me with his garment,
> and possessed me by his light....
> And the Lord (is) like the sun
> upon the face of the land.
> My eyes were enlightened,
> and my face received the dew. (11:11, 13–14)
> As the sun is the joy to them who seek its daybreak,
> so is my joy the Lord;
> because he is my sun,
> and his rays have restored me;
> and his light has dismissed all darkness from my face. (15:1–2)
> Let not light be conquered by darkness,
> nor let truth flee from falsehood. (18:6)
> A lamp you set for me both on my right and on my left,
> so that there might not be in me anything that is not light. (25:7)

Hating People

The same Qumran scroll that teaches hatred of "all the sons of darkness" paints a graphic picture of the struggle between good and evil in the world.[A-6] "Everlasting hatred" is part of the present world until the final age. This may be seen as justifying hatred of evil people:

> The nature of all the children of men is ruled by these (two spirits), and during their life all the hosts of men have a portion in their divisions and walk in (both) their ways. And the whole reward for their deeds shall be, for everlasting ages, according to whether each man's portion in their two divisions is great or small. For God has established the spirits in equal measure until the final age, and has set everlasting hatred between their divisions. Truth abhors the works of falsehood, and falsehood hates all the ways of truth. And their struggle is fierce in all their arguments for they do not walk together.[A-7]

"The Father loves the Son and has placed everything in his hands" (John 3:35). "For the Father loves the Son and shows him all he does" (5:20). He reaffirmed love in the way he loved others, whether friends like Martha, Mary, and Lazarus (11:5); or lost souls like the rich young ruler (Mark 10:21); or his close disciples (John 13:1).

Jesus also taught his disciples to love others as he had loved them. He illustrated this by washing their feet (John 13:1–17). Jesus even termed his teaching a new command: "A new command I give you: Love one another. As I have loved you, so you must love one another" (13:34). The primary background for John's talk of a "new" command in 1 John may well be Jesus on the night he was betrayed.

Its truth (2:8). See comments on 2 John 1.

In the light (2:9). See "The True Light."

Hates his brother (2:11). Jesus cited popular opinion that honoring God and hating certain people were compatible: "You have heard that it was said, 'Love your neighbor and hate your enemy'" (Matt. 5:43). Jesus rejected this, and so does John. But not all religious teachers of the time thought that hatred was necessarily a bad thing. *The Community Rule* of the Qumran community (CD 1.9–11) teaches that community members are to "love all the sons of light, each one according to his lot in God's plan, and to detest all the sons of darkness, each one in accordance to his blame in God's vindication." This hatred could be seen as a reflection of God's own loathing of evil; since God abhors the wickedness of the world, his people would be justified in

"STILL IN THE DARKNESS. . ."

abhorring wicked people (see "Hating People," below). In contrast to this John's teaching focuses on love and leaves judgment in God's hands.

John's teaching is unique here in the way it is grounded in the love shown in the death of Jesus Christ. But the notion that one should love one's enemies, or at least be kind to them, was present in Judaism long before New Testament times. For example, the *Letter of Aristeas* (170 B.C.?) describes a (probably fictitious) banquet in which an Egyptian king poses difficult questions to Jewish scholars.[38] One of the questions is, "To whom must a man be generous?" The answer is, first, that one should be magnanimous to friends, which is called "the general opinion." But like Jesus, though for different reasons, the Jewish scholar takes the matter a step farther: "My belief is that we must also show liberal charity to our opponents so that in this manner we may convert them to what is proper and fitting to them."

To the question, "To whom must one show favor?" the same Jew replies, "To his parents, always, for God's very great commandment concerns the honor due to parents. Next (and closely connected) [God] reckons the honor due to friends, calling the friend an equal of one's own self. You do well if you bring all men into friendship with yourself." If this is not identical to 1 John's appeal to love one's brother and not hate, it is at least consistent with John's thrust.

"THE WORLD AND ITS DESIRES..."

Roman gold coins with images of the emperors.

The evil one (2:13–14). This refers to the angelic being spoken of elsewhere in John as the devil, Satan, or "the prince of this world."[39] Jesus said that with his death and resurrection the power of the evil one is broken (12:31); he has "no hold" on Jesus (14:30). Yet until Christ returns, Satan makes trouble in the world and in the church by deceiving people and by spawning the lies and murderousness that are his trademarks. Satan is referred to in the Old Testament and frequently in Jewish literature of the New Testament era, often under the name Belial ("the worthless one") or Beliar, an evil being who orchestrates the workings of evil people. No wonder John's letter commends Christians who by faith in Christ "have overcome" this shadowy figure.

Do not love the world (2:15). Philo concurs: "It is impossible for love of the world to coexist with love for God, just as it is impossible for light and darkness to be present at the same time."[40] Philo traces the incessant wars of his age to one common source: "the desire of money, or fame, or pleasure. For the human race has its heart set on these things."[41] Many ancient authors speak of the evil in the world and how best to escape its consequences (see "Salvation from the World," below).

The world and its desires pass away (2:17). John's insight that the things of the world are not ultimate is important but far from unique. The third-century A.D. philosopher Porphyry commends a

▸ Salvation from the World

According to a Qumran document "The Wicked and the Holy" (4Q181), it is God who calls "sons of the world" into eternal life:

In accordance with the mercies of God, according to His goodness and wonderful glory, He caused some of the sons of the world to draw near (Him) . . . to be counted with Him in the com[munity of the g]ods as a congregation of holiness in service for eternal life and (sharing) the lot of His holy ones . . . each man according to his lot which He has cast for . . . eternal life.[A-8]

life of self-contentment rather than pursuit of luxury, for riches and fame bring nothing but problems.[42] Other pagan thinkers voice the same conviction.[43] The Hellenistic Jewish writer Philo, reflecting Stoic values, writes, "One should practice being contented with a little, for this is being near God; but the contrary habit is being very far from him."[44]

More distinctive is John's view of time.[45] The world is passing away; things are not an endless cycle. History is moving toward a grand goal. John is convinced that with Christ's coming it is now "the last hour" (2:18). This is the sense in which the world is passing away. He is not saying that created reality, or existence itself, can somehow disappear. It is rather that with Christ's coming the redemption of the world, the dawn of the long-awaited age to come, has moved a quantum leap closer. What that means is one of the subjects of the next section.

Key Counsel: Remain in His Anointing and Receive Eternal Life (2:18–3:8)

Dear children (2:18). John has feelings of affection for those he addresses. The religion he champions is a personal relationship with God through Jesus Christ (see 1:3). This God is known personally and intimately, cares for each of his worshipers, and unites them to other community members in a bond of love. Such a doctrine was virtually unknown in Greco-Roman religion. Albert A. Bell Jr. comments that the Egyptian goddess Isis "is virtually the only ancient divinity who displays any love or concern for her devotees."[46] But this did not translate into a community whose members' high calling was to love one another. The blessings of the mythological Isis pale in comparison to the promises of the real-world, incarnate Christ.

While John's language points to a stance of love for those he addresses, Stoic philosophy of the day reflected a different ideal. Life's goal was not to be united with others but to be free from the demands they might make. For the Roman moralist Seneca "not to be disturbed" was a high priority—to know "tranquillity of mind."[47] In Epictetus's teaching this called for maintaining distance from people and not being too attached to them—not even to wife and children.[48] Very different is the Christian mandate of loving others (as John evidently cares for his "dear children") and finding joy even in sacrifice for them.

Antichrist is coming (2:18). "Christ" means "Messiah," God's Anointed One, the deliverer of God's people. Among Jews and Christians of the first century was a wide range of messianic beliefs. Jesus warned his disciples about "false Christs" (Matt. 24:24). His disciples, who expected Christ himself to appear again to usher in the final age, taught that before he returned a sinister figure would arise, who would exalt himself against God and Christ's kingdom (2 Thess. 2:1–12). In all likelihood this is the shadowy "antichrist" of whom John speaks. In fact, he is already present in the form of "many antichrists," presumably enemies of the Jesus Christ preached by John and the other apostles.

Early Christian writers identified this antichrist in various ways. Polycarp (early 2d century) has a threefold description of such a figure.[49] He first quotes 1 John (cf. 1 John 4:2–3): "For every one who shall not confess that Jesus Christ is come in the flesh, is antichrist." He then issues two parallel warnings: "Whosoever shall not confess the testimony of the Cross, is of the devil; and whosoever shall pervert the oracles of the Lord to his own lusts and say that there is neither resurrection nor judgment, that man is the first-born of Satan." It is clear that early Christians kept their eyes open for opponents of Christ and the Christian message. The expectation of a satanic usurper of God's earthly kingdom is widespread in both ancient Christian (see "The Deceiver of the World," below) and Jewish apocalyptic writings.

They went out from us (2:19). Despite Jesus' stress on love and unity (e.g., John 13:34–35), the early church experienced frequent disagreement (e.g., Acts 15) and even open division. In the church at Ephesus (where the apostle John was active) late in the first century, there were "wicked men . . . who claim to be apostles but are not" (Rev. 2:2). False teachers also appear to have been a problem at the nearby churches of Pergamum (2:14–15) and Thyatira (2:20). As John writes 1 John, he is apparently aware that there has been schism in the congregation or congregations he addresses. This is lamentable.

But John sees it as evidence that those who have departed have never truly embraced the gospel to begin with: "If they had belonged to us, they would have remained with us" (1 John 2:19). Unity is a high priority, but even higher is fidelity to the apostolic message that "Jesus is the

The Deceiver of the World

John's reference to the Antichrist seems to be paralleled by a (slightly later?) early Christian writing that issues the following warning (see *Didache* 16:3–5):

For in the last days the false prophets and corrupters will abound, and the sheep will be turned into wolves, and love will be turned into hate. For as lawlessness increases, they will hate and persecute and betray one another. And then the deceiver of the world will appear as a son of God and will "perform signs and wonders" [Mark 13:22], and the earth will be delivered into his hands, and he will commit abominations the likes of which have never happened before. Then all humankind will come to the fiery test, and "many will fall away" and perish; but "those who endure" in their faith "will be saved" [cf. Matt. 24:10, 13].

Christ" (2:22). It is likely that John sees the division that has occurred as necessary because those who have departed physically have already departed from the Christian message doctrinally and ethically.

You have an anointing (2:20). In the days of Moses fine olive oil was rubbed or poured on objects to mark them off for God's special use. Aaron and his sons were anointed in this fashion for their service in the Tent of Meeting. This designated them as "a priesthood that will continue for all generations to come" (Ex. 40:15). Later in the history of Israel, prophets like Samuel anointed men chosen by God to be king. David was honored in this way; on that occasion the Holy Spirit "came upon David in power" (1 Sam. 16:13). Still later, and in John's own lifetime, Jesus Christ, the Son of David, was viewed by the early Christians as God's Anointed One par excellence (Acts 4:26; cf. Ps. 2:2).

As John writes to believers who "have an anointing," he has in mind this heritage of blessing and setting apart for service dating back many centuries to God's people in Old Testament times. The climactic coming of the "Anointed One" (*christos* in Greek, from which we get the word "Christ") results in a whole community who revel in the "anointing" that faith in Christ bestows. While some have recently departed from the Christian community (1 John 2:19), John addresses those who remain. From "the Holy One" (which can refer to either God or Christ) they have been gifted with the saving gospel message, the Holy Spirit, and baptism. As they remain true to the apostolic teaching in which John's letter confirms them, their "anointing" will keep them pointed in the right direction.[50]

The truth (2:20–21). See comments on 2 John 1.

What you have heard from the beginning (2:24). See comments on 1:1.

He promised us . . . eternal life (2:25). Clearly John views "eternal life" as an incentive to remain faithful. The words suggest to Christians the promise of heaven, and rightly so. One of the New Testament's best-known verses promises "eternal life" to all who place full personal trust in Jesus Christ (John 3:16), and Christ himself promised to prepare a place for his followers where they would join him in the afterlife (14:1–3).

But eternal life is more than something for later, after we die. It is for now. In John's time—and here our world is hardly different—life is constantly overshadowed by the threat of death. Coping mechanisms have to be devised. One notable philosophical response was denial, or more precisely apathy—a posture of resolute indifference to the surrounding world. This is seen in Epictetus's strategy of pretending that death is not what troubles people; it is rather the idea of death (see "Dealing with Death"). At work here is the belief that all reality is interconnected and material; life is a never-ending cycle of recurrence, in which there is no transcendent good or evil or indeed eternal meaning of any kind. Seneca's description of people illustrates this: "Born from nothingness they go back to nothingness" (*On Tranquillity of Mind* 15.4). We must therefore simply live in accordance with this inexorable natural flow. Meanwhile, within ourselves we work to stay insulated from pain and grief. Insulation is necessary because "the future, either in this life or after it, is nothing to look forward to."[51]

John, however, proclaims "the eternal life, which was with the Father and has appeared to us" (1 John 1:2). There *is* hope for the future![52] Obviously John points to Jesus Christ, who spoke of himself as "the resurrection and the life" and stated that whoever believes in him "will live, even though he dies" (John 11:25). But eternal life denotes more than the excellence and longevity of life with God in the age to come. It involves a spiritual quality of life in the here and now, a personal relationship with the Lord through faith.

Jesus illustrated eternal life not merely by alluding to heaven but also by pointing back to Moses' day. Just as the children of Israel lived by looking in faith on the bronze serpent displayed on a pole, so hearers of the gospel message "have eternal life" by looking in faith upon "the Son of Man . . . lifted up" (John 3:14–15; see "[Eternal] Life in Old Testament"). While Old Testament believers did not have specific knowledge of all points of Christian doctrine, New Testament writers see the offer of salvation extended in Old Testament times as a precedent for the gospel message now being preached.

For this reason, the words "live" and "life" in certain Old Testament contexts reverberate with the promise of "eternal life" sounded by John in 1 John 2:25. Notable examples are found especially in Deuteronomy.[53] Most telling here is 30:6: "The LORD your God will circumcise your hearts and the hearts of your descendants, so that you may love him with all your heart and with all your soul, and *live*" (italics added). Talk of circumcised hearts and of loving God with all one's heart and soul is, of course, language familiar to New Testament believers. It is the language of eternal life, God's covenant blessing, in the here and now.

Although John's letters have few direct references to the Old Testament, John (who was himself a Jew) has been educated in the synagogue. He has heard Jesus teach extensively from the Old Testament. He has heard Jesus tell skeptical detractors, "If you believed Moses, you would believe me, for he wrote about me" (John 5:46). John's Gospel also records Jesus' words "salvation is from the Jews" (4:22). It is little surprise, then, that the primary background for understanding "life" as the eternal God bestows it in salvation through Christ, or "eternal life," is the Hebrew Scriptures and the history of Israel.

Anointing (2:27). See comments on 2:20.

Dealing with Death

The gospel message promises eternal life, meaning a transformed "now" as well as a glorious "hereafter." Death has been defeated by Christ. Very different is the vision set forth by the Stoic writer Epictetus, which does not so much face death as deny it:[A-9]

When you see a person weeping in sorrow for a child gone abroad or dead, or for loss of his property, take care that the appearances do not carry you away, as if he were suffering in external things. Make a distinction in your own mind and say, "It is not what happened that afflicts this man, but it is the opinion about that thing that afflicts the man." So far as words, then, do not be unwilling to show him sympathy, and even to lament with him. But take care that you do not lament in your inner being also.

(Eternal) Life in the Old Testament

Jesus taught Nicodemus about eternal life by reminding him of an incident that took place in Moses' day (John 3:10–15). There the people "lived"—were spared God's judgment and could enjoy covenant blessings—by heeding the message Moses proclaimed to them.

They traveled from Mount Hor along the route to the Red Sea, to go around Edom. But the people grew impatient on the way; they spoke against God and against Moses, and said, "Why have you brought us up out of Egypt to die in the desert? There is no bread! There is no water! And we detest this miserable food!" Then the LORD sent venomous snakes among them; they bit the people and many Israelites died. The people came to Moses and said, "We sinned when we spoke against the LORD and against you. Pray that the LORD will take the snakes away from us." So Moses prayed for the people. The LORD said to Moses, "Make a snake and put it up on a pole; anyone who is bitten can look at it and live." So Moses made a bronze snake and put it up on a pole. Then when anyone was bitten by a snake and looked at the bronze snake, he lived. (Num. 21:4–9)

Do not need anyone to teach you (2:27). In part this is a figure of speech; King Agrippa uses it in a letter to Josephus.[54] If his audience literally needed no instruction, John would not be writing.

Children of God (3:1–2). In broad terms all humankind are children of God in that God is their Maker (Isa. 45:11–12). More particularly, Israel has God as its Father (Deut. 32:6ff.; Isa. 43:6–7). But Christians are children of God in a still fuller sense: Christ has given to those who believe in him "the right to become children of God—children born not of natural descent, nor of human decision or a husband's will, but born of God" (John 1:12–13).

Human fathers in the Greco-Roman world had the power of life and death over children. They were not always affectionate or even equitable. Children were unwanted in many quarters of the classical world. When they were born, a father was free to order them to be "exposed"—that is, taken to an out-of-the-way place and left to die. The church father Tertullian notes that under the proconsulship of Tiberius in north Africa, children were sacrificed to Saturn; across the empire children were killed "by drowning, or by exposure to cold and hunger and dogs."[55] Childhood was by no means always a time of safety and nurture in such an age. Nor is it today, with child neglect a perennial problem and abortion on demand an international, and especially American, disgrace (see "Tertullian on Abortion," below).

How different from heartless human parents is the heavenly Father, who has "lavished" love on his children (3:1) both in this world and in the next, when "we shall be like him, for we shall see him as he is" (3:2). This sure hope moves God's children to purify themselves, "just as he is pure" (3:3). In this they are assured of success because Christ has been successful in his mission "to destroy the devil's work" (3:8).

Do not let anyone lead you astray (3:7). John writes to protect his readers against false teachers, teachings, and practices. In Old Testament times idolatry misled many (Deut. 13:6; 2 Kings 21:9). The subversion of God's people by evil angelic beings is a recurrent theme of later Jewish literature as well (*1 Enoch* 6–10, *Jub.* 5:1–10). *Testament of Levi* 10:2 and 16:1, in warning of end-time transgression, use a word related to John's "lead astray." John is warning of missteps that can have consequences of eschatological proportions.

Son of God (3:8). See also comments on "children of God" at 3:10. "Son of God" is the title for Jesus Christ that occurs most frequently in the Johannine letters.[56] Its shortened version "Son" is even more common.[57] It refers to Jesus' divinity, his unique oneness with God the Father. In Hellenistic religion there was talk of divine sonship via human cohabitation with a god; the offspring would be a "son of a god." Caesar Augustus was thought to have divine parentage as the result of his mother's impregnation by a snake in the temple of Apollo.[58] In a religious setting where the gods were both numerous and essentially human in their characteristics, the notion of a human attaining some semblance of divinity is hardly startling.

Very different is the idea of Jesus' divine sonship. He is the only Son (John 1:18: Gk. *monogenēs hyios*) of the "God" who is "holy"—utterly unique. His conception by the Holy Spirit was without male human agency. His relationship to God is unparalleled because he had been "with God" and "came from God" in a sense true of no other human being (1:1; 8:42). He was sinless. He fully shared our lot but at the same time transcended it. No wonder he (and only he) is able, as 1 John 3:8 says, "to destroy the devil's work."

The devil (3:8). See comments on 2:13–14.

REFLECTIONS

IT HAS BEEN NOTED THAT "CLEARLY WITHOUT BELIEF in God sin has no meaning."[A-10] For increasing numbers of people in postmodern society, the classical Christian idea of God is on the wane. The consciousness of sin likewise diminishes.

Even where sin is recognized, it may be rationalized as inhabiting only the most depraved few (Hitler, Stalin, serial killers, etc.), as being solely the product of social conditioning; or as being only a cultural perception when in fact there is no right or wrong. In some understandings sin is ignorance; therefore education is the answer to personal and social problems. Others believe that medicine, especially behavior-modifying drugs, hold the answer to "sin" (to the extent there is such a thing). One of the most popular responses to sin, in all ages, is denial, grounded in that most persistent of all human character traits: proud self-righteousness.

We all must admit that life has its gray areas. But if the Bible's commands articulate valid standards of God's character and prescriptions for people's attitudes and behavior, gray areas are the exception and not the rule. Christ came to take away our sin, not make us experts in self-justification or sin management. The power that raised him from the dead can fill our lives with the desire to move toward a higher plane on which Christ's commands become our goal and delight.

Statement of the Letter's Central Warning: Beware Cain's Error and False Prophets (3:9–4:6)

In this section John uses the negative example of Cain to warn his readers of certain dangers they face—especially the danger of lovelessness. He then reminds them, once again, of the love command and urges them to scrutinize the beliefs, ideas, and practices they adopt. Such scrutiny is necessary because "many false prophets have gone out into the world" (4:1).

God's seed (3:9). Other writers recognize that what is true and noble within persons is the result of divine implantation (see "Saving Understanding" at 5:20, in which Philo speaks of God sowing virtues in humankind). Biblical writers tend to speak of the implantation of the divine word (see James 1:18, 21).

Cannot go on sinning (3:9). The Roman moralist Seneca attributes virtuous behavior to the power of human goodness. Virtuous action comes from within and by one's own volition. Seneca speaks of "the man of perfect wisdom," who is impervious to lapses of good judgment and behavior.[59] As an example he points to Horatius Cocles, a mythical one-eyed military leader of Rome's early history, who modeled consistency and was good, not by dint of conscious planning but simply because that was his character. "Moral perfection" was recognizable in him, Seneca concludes.[60]

John refers not to human virtue in the Greco-Roman sense but to compliance with God's law (3:4) and conformity to Jesus' daily walk (2:6). This is possible only because of spiritual new birth, which John calls being "born of God" (3:9). It is unlikely that John has in mind absolute sinless perfection, since earlier he has denounced those who say they are without sin (1:8, 10). Rather, John has in mind the blatant sinning to which those who have left the community have fallen prey (2:19). In view of the letter as a whole, such sinning probably involves denial of Christ's human nature (4:2–3; theological lapse), flaunting of God's (or Christ's) commands (2:4; ethical lapse), failure to love (4:20; relational lapse), or some combination of these grave errors.

We know who the children of God are (3:10). See comments on 3:1–2. The first-century rhetorician Dio Chrysostom records a conversation between the Cynic philosopher Diogenes and Alexander the Great.[61] The latter asked the Cynic his opinion of the claim of some that Alexander was begotten by a god. Diogenes's reply was that if Alexander lived in a disciplined fashion and showed understanding of "the divine art of being king," then nothing prevented Alexander from being "a son of Zeus."[62]

Like Diogenes, John sees a connection between human behavior and divine

Tertullian on Abortion

"Children of God" in Christ can count on faithful love and protection from their heavenly Father. In the ancient world Greco-Roman fathers sometimes set a very different family tone. Children were destroyed in the womb if they were unwanted or illegitimate. The early Christian leader Tertullian protested this and described the contrasting behavior of Christians:

> In our case, murder being once for all forbidden, we may not destroy even the fetus in the womb, while as yet the human being derives blood from others parts of the body for its sustenance. To hinder a birth is merely a speedier man-killing; nor does it matter whether you take away a life that is born, or destroy one that is coming to the birth. That is a man which is going to be one; you have the fruit already in its seed.[A-11]

▸Josephus on Cain

John's letter limits its criticism of Cain to the murder of Abel recorded in Genesis 4. Josephus extends the condemnation considerably:

> Even while Adam was alive, it came to pass that the posterity of Cain became exceeding wicked, every one successively dying one after another more wicked than the former. They were intolerable in war, and vehement in robberies; and if anyone were slow to murder people, yet was he bold in his profligate behavior, in acting unjustly and doing injuries for gain.[A-12]

blessing. But "God" for John is not Zeus, part of the Greco-Roman pantheon of gods and goddesses. Consequently, John calls for doing "what is right"—that is, living in keeping with the nature and commandments of the God whom Jesus revealed. Likewise, John calls for love for others—something fundamentally characteristic of the Hebrew-Christian God but alien to the nature of the deities of the Greco-Roman religion. "Children of God" in John's sense and a "son of Zeus" in Diogenes's sense are actually two very different things.

Children of the devil (3:10). See comments on "the evil one" at 2:13–14; 5:19. Just as a child of God is someone who reflects his or her divine parentage by embodying the heavenly Father's goodness (see Eph. 5:1–2), a child of the devil is someone who practices Satan's deceit and ill will toward God and fellow humans.

SYNAGOGUE
The fourth-century A.D. Jewish synagogue at Sardis.

Do not be like Cain (3:12). In the twentieth century names like Stalin, Pol Pot, and Hitler became synonymous with murderous intrigue and social chaos. In ancient Jewish literature Cain played a similar role. Why was he so despised? Philo thinks Cain's sin lay in his focus on "earthly and inanimate things," his love for himself, and his offhand attitude toward God's standards of acceptable sacrifices.[63] For Philo virtue lies in attention to the things of the soul, not of the earth. Josephus accuses Cain of greed and of impropriety in plowing the earth; this meant that the sacrifice he offered to God was "forced from nature by the ingenuity of grasping man."[64] He introduced great evil into the world by "rapine and violence"; further, he corrupted "that simplicity in which men lived before by the invention of weights and measures: the guileless and generous existence which they had enjoyed in ignorance of these things he converted into a life of craftiness."[65]

Genesis 4:1–16 relates the original story of Cain's slaughter of his brother Abel. John's critique of Cain is simple: He murdered Abel because of jealousy. Abel's sacrifice was acceptable to God, and Cain's sacrifice was rejected. Cain's behav-

Ben Sirach on Almsgiving

Christians should be exemplary in their love for each other, John teaches. This love must not be mere words but extend to deeds and physical goods (3:17). The second-century B.C. Jewish writing quoted below sounds similar notes. It is different from Christian writings in that it forbids giving alms to "the sinner." Also, it suggests that almsgiving atones for sin (Sir. 3:30). John presents Christian love as a response to God's grace, not a means of acquiring that grace.

> If you do good, know to whom you do it,
> and you will be thanked for your good deeds.
> Do good to the devout, and you will be repaid—
> if not by them, certainly by the Most High.
> No good comes to the one who persists in evil
> or to one who does not give alms.
> Give to the devout, but do not help the sinner.
> Do good to the humble, but do not give to the ungodly;
> hold back their bread, and do not give it to them,
> for by means of it they might subdue you;
> then you will receive twice as much evil
> for all the good you have done to them.
> For the Most High also hates sinners
> and will inflict punishment on the ungodly.
> Give to the one who is good, but do not help the sinner. (12:1–7)

ior and underlying attitude were the utter antithesis of love. John uses Cain, the epitome of treachery, as an example of how God's people must *not* regard each other. Christian faith generates active goodwill for others, not murderous impulses toward them. Christians know they "have passed from death to life" (1 John 3:14) because they love each other rather than despise each other or remain indifferent to a brother or sister in need.

Hates his brother (3:15). Seneca frankly points out how "hatred of the human race seizes us" because of the corruption and foolishness we see on every hand. But his strategy for coping with it is as flimsy as it is surprising: Laugh! Scoff and be cynical! "Therefore all things must be made light of and borne with a calm mind. It is more manlike to scoff at life than to bewail it."[66] Seneca's frankness is admirable, but John points to a better solution in 3:16.

Eternal life (3:15). See comments on 2:25.

Jesus Christ laid down his life for us. And we ought . . . (3:16). Whereas Seneca prescribed cynicism as an antidote for hatred of others (see comments on 3:15), John calls for attention to Christ's saving death. The cross, which is our only ground for salvation, summons those it saves to take up their cross in seeking the good of others. Just as Jesus prayed for his enemies and could therefore intercede for them even as they willed his death (Luke 23:34), so his followers can learn to walk in love where otherwise they might harbor malice.

Give to Needy Brothers

In language similar to that found in John's letter, the Old Testament calls on the people of God to extend physical aid to needy brethren.

If there is a poor man among your brothers in any of the towns of the land that the LORD your God is giving you, do not be hardhearted or tightfisted toward your poor brother. Rather be openhanded and freely lend him whatever he needs. . . . Give generously to him and do so without a grudging heart; then because of this the LORD your God will bless you in all your work and in everything you put your hand to. (Deut. 15:7–8, 10)

If anyone has material possessions . . . but has no pity (3:17). Jewish religion of the first century went to great lengths to care for the poor. Josephus boasted that "no Jew depended on outsiders for charitable support, since the Jews cared for all of their destitute and disabled brethren."[67] Writers like Ben Sirach extolled the virtues of giving to the needy (almsgiving). Yet only good people ought to receive charitable aid (see "Ben Sirach on Almsgiving").

This then is how we know that we belong to the truth (3:19). If "this then" refers back to preceding verses (esp. to 3:18), John seems to be linking Christian assurance to ethical behavior. If we love in deed and not word alone, our standing before God is confirmed. It is always tempting to think we are right with God when our hearts are in fact hardened toward him, as revealed by lack of compassion for others. An Old Testament background for John's teaching here is likely (see "Give to Needy Brothers").[68]

QUMRAN

Cave 4—the principal cave for the discovery of many of the Dead Sea Scrolls.

Truth (3:19). See comments on 2 John 1.

False prophets (4:1). In Greco-Roman religion of the time there was high interest in secret or privileged knowledge of supernatural mysteries. There was "proliferation of personal dream revelations, oracles and their interpretation, magic and astrology"; further, there were "numerous exclusive groups offering initiates higher knowledge for their personal weal and salvation."[69] A Roman military leader kept a Syrian prophetess named Martha with his army to furnish advice on important decisions; the Roman senate itself might settle an issue according to the prophetic pronouncement of a priest or priestess.[70] In Jewish settings both Philo and Josephus warn against false prophets.[71]

Jesus Christ has come in the flesh (4:2). On the rise of docetic views of Christ, see comments on Cerinthus and Gnosticism under "Challenges Confronting the Churches" in the introduction.

Spirit of truth (4:6). See comments at 2 John 1.

Foundational Assurance: God's Love (4:7–14)

Thus far John has focused on statements of fact about God, on various commands and counsel, and on necessary warnings. In this section he repeats these themes but shifts the emphasis slightly to concentrate on the love of God shown in the sacrifice of Christ.

Let us love one another (4:7). See comments on 2:5, 7, 8, 11, 18.

God is love (4:8). He is not *only* love, of course; one listing arrives at 152 different "designations, descriptions, and figures of speech for God" in the Bible![72]

Yet a foundational tenet of Old Testament theology is that the God of Abraham, Isaac, and Jacob is a God who zealously loves his people. Moses composed a hymn to God that stated, "In your unfailing love you will lead the people you have redeemed" (Ex. 15:13). Although he punishes rebellion, God shows "love to a thousand generations of those" who turn to him in faith (20:6). When Moses was granted a glimpse of the distant edge of God's glory, the heavenly voice he heard affirmed: "The LORD, the LORD, the compassionate and gracious God, slow to anger, abounding in love and faithfulness, maintaining love to thousands, and forgiving wickedness, rebellion and sin" (34:6–7). The Psalms reverberate with affirmations of God's love. Prophets like Isaiah and Hosea repeatedly extol it.

The covenant love of God is one of the most prevalent themes of all three divisions of the Hebrew Bible—Law, Prophets, Writings. This same God "showed his love among us" (1 John 4:9) in Christ.

In Greco-Roman religion there were many gods, with diverse qualities, so one

Seneca's Theology of Despair

John affirms that God is love. He has shown this by sending "his one and only Son into the world that we might live through him" (4:9). God, love, and life are closely linked.

Very different is the "god" of Seneca and of Stoic philosophy popular among many first-century intellectuals. This god admits that sometimes life is tough. But he advises suffering humans to respond to hardship with scornful indifference. And if this is not enough, why, die at your own hand! John's assurance regarding the God who knows us personally and loves us and gives us life, and Seneca's cold depiction of a god totally indifferent to whether people live or die, could not be more antithetical.

["God" says:] Yes . . . I have armed your minds to withstand [all sorrows]; endure with fortitude. Scorn poverty; no one lives as poor as he was born. Scorn pain; it will either be relieved or relieve you. Scorn death, which either ends you or transfers you. . . . Above all, I have taken pains that nothing should keep you here against your will; the way out lies open. . . . Death lies near at hand. . . . Anywhere you wish, the way is open. Even that which we call dying, the moment when the breath forsakes the body, is so brief that its fleetness cannot come within the ken. Whether the throat is strangled by a knot, or water stops the breathing, or the hard ground crushes in the skull of one falling headlong to its surface, or flame inhaled cuts off the course of respiration—be it what it may, the end is swift. Do you not blush for shame? You dread so long what comes so quickly![A-13] could not say that the gods were of any particular single quality (except maybe unpredictable). Moreover, where Stoicism held sway, even when "god" (Latin *deus*) is spoken of in the singular, he is subject to a force greater than he is: fate. Seneca writes, "Although the great creator and ruler of the universe himself wrote the decrees of Fate, yet he follows them. . . . It is impossible for the moulder to alter matter; to this law it [i.e., the god] has submitted."[73] No picture of God as being love, or even expressing love, can be glimpsed here. In fact, in one remarkable passage Seneca represents "god" as inviting people who encounter sorrows and hardships just to be tough and scorn it all; if that doesn't work, commit suicide! (see "Seneca's Theology of Despair").

He sent his . . . Son . . . that we might live (4:9). Christ brings life; Greco-Roman gods might encourage death (see "Seneca's Theology of Despair"). In any case no pagan gods came as a real human being (like Jesus of Nazareth), died a sacrifice for sin, and rose from the dead to ensure (eternal) life.

Not that we loved God (4:10). Many Jewish sources appear to portray God's love as the result of some merit on our part. Philo speaks of a sect called the Therapeutae, whose "virtue . . . has procured [for] them his [i.e., God's] love as their most appropriate reward."[74] Another source states, "God loves nothing so much as the person who lives with wisdom."[75] God "will love you more than does your mother" if you are "like a father to orphans" (Sir. 4:10). It is important to visit the sick "because for such deeds you will be loved [by God]. In all you do, remember the end of your life, and then you will never sin" (Sir. 7:35–36).

But John grounds God's love not in human virtue or meritorious acts (as important as good works are for John), but in Christ's "atoning sacrifice for our sins" (1 John 4:10; see comments on 2:1). The background for John's understanding of atoning sacrifice is clearly the Old Testament sacrificial system as fulfilled in the crucifixion of Jesus.

ALTAR OF BURNT SACRIFICE

A model of the altar in the Court of Priests in the Jerusalem Temple.

Since God so loved us, we also ought to love one another (4:11). Since Old Testament times God has called on his people to reflect his character: "Be holy, because I am holy" (Lev. 11:45). The call to love is no less binding than the call to holiness. Here too is a noteworthy link between John and Paul, who wrote to the Ephesians (among whom John later served as pastor): "Be imitators of God, therefore, as dearly loved children and live a life of love, just as Christ loved us and gave himself up for us" (Eph. 5:1–2).

We have seen (4:14). See comments on 1:1.

Necessary Instruction: Believing in Jesus the Christ, the Son of God (4:15–5:15)

In the Greek text 80 percent of the occurrences of the words "believe" or "faith" in 1 John occur in this section of the letter. John moves to express in a more didactic way matters that he touched on in the form of commands, counsel, warnings, or assurance in previous sections.

Rely on the love God has for us (4:16). This can also be translated, "Believe the love that God has for us." God's love is of no saving effect if the sinner is not inclined to desire and reciprocate it. Numerous Old Testament passages lament that God's people, to whom he extended himself in love, would "not listen," much less return his affection.[76]

God is love (4:16). See comments on 4:8.

Confidence on the day of judgment (4:17). According to *1 Enoch*, judgment will be a horror for many: "But the Lord of the Spirits himself will cause them to be frantic, so that they shall rush and depart from his presence. Their faces shall be filled with shame, and their countenances shall be crowned with darkness."[77] Jesus warned of a time of "weeping and gnashing of teeth" (Matt. 8:12; 25:30).

But John holds forth confidence on the last day because of the work of God's love among his people, and because they have allowed themselves to be conformed to him (1 John 4:17: "In this world we are like him"; cf. 2:6). God's love is not just to be admired at a distance; it aims to transform the lives of those it touches and give them hope.

No fear in love (4:18). Pagan writers of antiquity recognized that servile fear of ruling authorities was an ineffective control measure. It was far better for rulers to cultivate the loyalty of love in their subjects. This would enhance attainment of both personal and societal goals, according to Cicero (first-century B.C.).[78] Another writer, Palladius of Alexandria (fourth century A.D.) recognizes that love involves trust, not anxiety and compulsion.[79] Love is free from fear in the sense of fawning insecurity or abject terror.

What is complex here is that there is both an *absence of fear* before God that "perfect love" for God casts out and an appropriate fear of God. An extreme example of the latter might be Uzzah's lack of fear in touching the ark of God, for which he was struck dead (2 Sam. 6:6–7).

John is apparently not speaking of that worshipful, awe-filled veneration of the God before whom the earth shakes, the positive "fear of the LORD" spoken of elsewhere in Scripture (e.g., Prov. 1:7; cf. Luke 12:5). A theologian of the Reformation era wrote, "The gist of true piety does not consist in a fear which would gladly flee the judgment of God, but . . . rather in a pure and true zeal which loves God altogether as Father, and reveres him

REFLECTIONS

DOES "WHOEVER LIVES IN LOVE, LIVES IN GOD" (4:16) perhaps imply that if a human being experiences love, he or she is experiencing God and therefore has no need to believe in Christ for salvation? For John the answer would seem to be no. "Love" in 1 John, as in John's Gospel, might be called "cruciform." That is, it is expressed in and defined by the cross of Jesus Christ. For John, to live in love means to believe in the crucified Christ for salvation, honoring his commands and learning to love his priorities in this world. Those without Christ may still experience the "love" of God's creation order. But they have not yet received the full measure of love that hearing and receiving the gospel bestows.

truly as Lord, embraces his justice and dreads to offend him more than to die."[80]

What John says here in no way rules out "fear of the Lord" defined as highest respect and worshipfulness in the presence of Almighty God.

Cannot love God, whom he has not seen (4:20). John's logic in this verse is profound, yet simple. Another first-century Jewish writer reflects a similar chain of thought: "And it is impossible that the invisible God can be piously worshipped by those people who behave with impiety toward those who are visible and near to them."[81] Plutarch wrote, regarding human relations in the family, that love among siblings is practically tantamount to love for parents.[82] This would imply that children of God, by loving one another, are already well on their way to showing the love for their Father that Scripture commands.

Children of God (5:2). See comments on 3:1–2.

This is love for God: to obey his commands (5:3). John proposes a two-way street between love and law. Love seeks to fulfill the law, while honoring the law is a means of expressing love (see "Love Instead of Law?"; see also comments on 2 John 6).

His commands are not burdensome (5:3). Even prior to Christ's coming there was awareness among God's people that relationship with the Lord is a matter of the heart and not just formal obedience to ponderous commands. For example, Tobit instructs his son Tobias, "So now, my child, remember these commandments, and do not let them be erased from your heart" (Tobit 4:19). Later Tobit affirms, "If you turn to him with all your heart and with all your soul, to do what is true before him, then he will turn to you and will no longer hide his face from you" (13:6). The touching Prayer of Manasseh (11–12) has the king of Judah praying, in view of his sins: "And now I bend the knee of my heart, imploring you for your kindness. I have sinned, O Lord, I have sinned, and I acknowledge my transgressions."

All of these accounts are fictitious, and none of them expresses the conviction and clarity of John's affirmation in 1 John 5:3. Yet all show an awareness of

▸ Love Instead of Law?

While John calls both for upholding the law and expressing love, a first-century writer under apparent Christian influence calls for meditation on God's love, not on the law (cf. Ps. 1:2). Other themes of 1 John that appear below: children of God, truth, faith, life, and light.

Let all the Lord's babes praise him,
and let us receive the truth of his faith.
And his children shall be acknowledged by him,
therefore let us sing of his love.

We live in the Lord by his grace,
and life we receive by his Messiah.
For a great day has shined upon us,
and wonderful is he who has given to us his glory.
Let us, therefore, all of us agree in the name of the Lord,
and let us honor him in his goodness.
And let our faces shine in his light,
and let our hearts meditate in his love,
by night and by day.[A-14]

a similar hope—a hope awaiting fulfillment at the coming of Christ—that the God who expresses himself in his law redeems people in their hearts so as to love and fulfill his will.

Came by water and blood (5:6). Jesus' identity is gauged by both his baptism ("water") and crucifixion ("blood"). The false teacher Cerinthus, followed by others, denied Jesus' essential deity. In this view Jesus was a normal man who received a special spiritual gift at his baptism. But he remained fully and only mortal. As a result it was not really God the Son who died on the cross, just a man who exemplified God in many ways (see "Irenaeus on Cerinthus" in the introduction).

John disagrees. Jesus' divine status was not merely conferred from the outside at his baptism, a view called adoptionism. Rather, from his very conception his relationship with God and origin in God marked him as unique, though fully sharing in the human condition. Jesus therefore "came," embodied and revealed God's presence, not only at his baptism by the Spirit (as Cerinthus argued) but also in his death on the cross. In his Son, God himself (and not merely a representative human) bore the penalty of human sinfulness. This is the saving truth of the gospel to which "the Spirit . . . testifies" (5:6).

The Spirit is the truth (5:6). See comments on "truth" at 2 John 1.

We accept man's testimony (5:9). See comments on 1:1. While ancient means of historical reporting sometimes lacked the precision of modern data collection, there was still concern for truth-telling in relating recollection of events. Josephus complains that some had written "histories" about the Roman war against Jerusalem around A.D. 70, but those persons had "never visited the sites nor were anywhere near the actions described, but, having put together a few hearsay reports . . . with the gross impudence of drunken revellers, miscalled their productions by the name of history."[83] To the extent that Josephus is right, John's statement rings true that if we give credence to human testimony, we ought to heed God all the more.

God's testimony is greater (5:9). During Jesus' earthly days he pointed to a rich fourfold divine witness to himself: John the Baptist's testimony, the miraculous works that Jesus performed, the Father's own testimony (at Jesus' baptism?), and the Scriptures (John 5:31–40).

Eternal life (5:11, 13). See comments on 2:25.

Have the Son . . . . believe in the name of the Son (5:12, 13). What is the most important thing in the pursuit of knowing God? For John, having the Son is foremost a matter of believing, of exercising faith in the apostolic proclamation about Jesus Christ's life, death, and resurrection (1:1–4).

THE JORDAN RIVER

Other writers of the time saw things differently. Philo extolled four virtues: wisdom, courage, temperance, and justice. These flow from the word of God in the form of doctrines that increase and nourish the "souls that love God."[84] Philo cannot be said to reject the notion of faith, but neither does it play an explicit prominent role in his writings. The writer of 1 Maccabees calls for faithfulness like Abraham's (not "faith," as Paul describes it in Abraham; see Rom. 4), whose obedience when he was ordered to slay Isaac "was reckoned to him as righteousness" (1 Macc. 2:52). Abraham's greatness lay in his obedience to the law (Sir. 44:20), not in the trust he placed in God's promise when all visible possibilities of the promise's fulfillment had vanished (cf. Paul's differing assessment in Rom. 4:20–22).

DEATH

Tombs in the necropolis at Hierapolis in Asia Minor.

John does not criticize virtues and commands—far from it. But he grounds salvation in Christ's work, not human actions. That is why the Son is central as the source of eternal life, and that is why believing in him is presented as the primary characteristic of the true child of God.

Ask . . . according to his will (5:14). In the prayers of Greco-Roman religion, "the attitude was that of self-interest."[85] Central was the will of the worshiper, not the will of the god or goddess being petitioned. In the Old Testament Apocrypha prayer is portrayed as a means of gleaning secret information from God for personal and political gain (Judith 11:17)—though to be sure, in many other passages in the Apocrypha, more noble views of prayer are suggested. Whereas John implies that God is anxious to hear our prayers because he is the loving Father of his children, the book of Tobit sees human merit as the key to successful prayer (see "Prayer and Good Works").

If we know he hears . . . we have what we ask (5:15). John was present the night Jesus prayed in Gethsemane (Matt.

Prayer and Good Works

In the Old Testament Apocrypha book of Tobit an angel gives the following instruction regarding prayer to Tobit and his son Tobias:

> Prayer is good when accompanied by fasting, almsgiving, and righteousness. A little with righteousness is better than much with wrongdoing. It is better to give alms than to treasure up gold. For almsgiving delivers from death, and it will purge away every sin. Those who perform deeds of charity and of righteousness will have fullness of life; but those who commit sin are the enemies of their own lives. (Tobit 12:8–10 RSV)

At the end of the book the aged and dying Tobit makes this observation: "See now, my children, consider what almsgiving accomplishes and how righteousness delivers" (14:11 RSV). In contrast to this, 1 John speaks of a confidence grounded in Christ's perfect sacrifice, not in our good works.

26:37). Jesus requested some way around "this cup"—the cross (26:39). Yet his highest desire was the Father's will, not his own (26:42). When we pray with that same confidence in the Father, and with abandonment of personal short-term gain, "we have what we asked from him" (1 John 5:15), which is the privilege of an audience with the Father, the confidence (5:14) of his listening ear, and the benefit of his all-wise decision. This decision may or may not correspond to what we in our human limitations would like to see happen.

Concluding Admonition: The True God and the Threat of Imposters (5:16–21)

In the letter's last six verses John touches in a summary way on themes he has already mentioned. These include love for others by praying for them (or not), the assurance of being children of God, and a final blanket imperative to avoid all God-substitutes.

A sin that does not lead to death (5:16). There is no one whose life is free of sin (see comments on 1:8). The only final remedy for sin is Jesus Christ (see comments on 2:1). But like his master Jesus, John believes in the power of prayer. Part of the ministry of prayer is supplication for others, even for their sins.

By "a sin that does not lead to death" John probably has in mind the full range of transgressions that even Christians may fall into. These can be serious. Note how Jesus prayed for Peter in advance of Peter's betrayal of him (Luke 22:32). He prayed for his persecutors at his crucifixion (23:34), a prayer that Stephen later echoed as he was being stoned to death (Acts 7:60). Paul prayed for the salvation of fellow Jews (Rom. 10:1). Yet if one scans the full range of New Testament prayers,[86] it is remarkable how few prayers are recorded for the forgiveness of sins of Christians. The assumption seems rather to be that Christians will be characterized by active obedience to God rather than chronic rebellion against him. Still, when Christians stumble, others should seek their restoration (Gal. 6:1). Prayer is an aspect of the ministry of restoration (Rom. 12:12: "Be . . . faithful in prayer"). We should also pray that we will not succumb to sin ourselves: "Pray that you will not fall into temptation" (Luke 22:40); "and lead us not into temptation" (Matt. 6:13).

Perhaps John would say that many sins that do not "lead to death" are to be dealt with in the daily course of confession and prayer by God's people, whether personally or together as the church (1 John 1:9). An example of Christians coming to grips with sin in their midst is found in 2 Corinthians 7:8–11. The Corinthians exercised the repentance (which implies prayer) "that leads to salvation." Their waywardness was serious, but it did not "lead to death" (i.e., irrevocable judgment at God's hand) in the end because they turned to God in prayer and adjusted their lives accordingly.

A sin that leads to death (5:16). John knew that even though Christ wept over Jerusalem (Luke 19:41) and in a sense died for all (1 John 2:2), not all will be saved. Even among those in the church, there are pretenders and deceivers (1 John 2:19; 4:1). John may be speaking here of sins that, if persisted in, will result in eternal judgment (see comments on 3:9; a biblical example is perhaps Esau; see Heb. 12:16–17). Those who "know him who is true" (5:20), by contrast, manifest signs of life rather than these symptoms of death.

I am not saying that he should pray about that (5:16). John does not forbid prayer for "sin that leads to death," but he does not command it. Perhaps this may be compared to God's command to Jeremiah not to pray for God's people who had so flagrantly turned aside from God's counsel (Jer. 7:16; 14:1). Apparently this was a temporary order, for God has to repeat it, and late in life Jeremiah is still interceding and receiving answer to his prayers (Jer. 42). But in times of spiritual deception, one may need to disengage emotionally from situations and relationships. Prayer involves an emotional engagement that can lead us past the point of legitimate intercession for others' forgiveness, to the dangerous point of sympathizing more with sinners in their rebellion than with God in his just enforcement of the terms of his promises.

Sometimes a situation has reached the point that the time for prayer has passed (Isa. 1:15; 16:12), even though that point may be tempered with God's rich mercy—as Abraham discovered when he pled for Sodom (Gen. 18:23–32) and as John himself discovered when he and his brother James wished to call down destroying fire from heaven (Luke 9:54–55). Jesus prayed before he chose Judas and later even washed his feet, but the time came when he had to let him go his own way (John 13:27).

In a word, as John addresses a church setting where some have fallen prey to the deception of the Antichrist, the evil one, he may be granting permission to commend the souls of some, whose separation from God seems to be terminal, into God's hands. This does not mean hate them. This does not mean that prayer cannot turn a sinner from his ways (James 5:16–20). But if one's spiritual rebellion leads him or her away from God and threatens to draw us away too, there may come a time to entrust such a person's soul to God and focus our worship and prayer on other matters, at least for a time.

Born of God (5:18). See comments on 3:1–2.

▸ Saving Understanding

For John the insight that mediates salvation comes from God and points to God's Son (5:20). Philo extols a different, philosophical understanding, praising that treasure-house

> in your own keeping, not where gold and silver, substances corruptible, are stored, but where lies that most beautiful of all possessions, the knowledge of the Cause and of virtue, and, besides these two, of the fruit which is engendered by them both.[A-15]

Philo agrees that this redemptive knowledge is from above—it is divinely implanted. But God's gift is not the gift of his Son but of virtues:

> A husband unites with his wife . . . in a union which tends to the generation of children, in strict accordance with and obedience to nature. But it is not lawful for virtues, which are the parents of many perfect things, to associate with a mortal husband. But they, without having received the power of generation from any other being, will never be able by themselves alone to conceive any thing. Who, then, is it who sows good seed in them, except the Father of the universe, the uncreated God, he who is the parent of all things?[A-16]

Under the control of the evil one (5:19). John has made it clear elsewhere that the Lord, not "the evil one," has ultimate control. By faith God's children are free from evil's dominion, "because the one who is in [believers] is greater than the one who is in the world" (4:4). Yet until Christ's return, the evil one (also called "antichrist" in 1 John) has a vast following (4:5). The world has the appearance of belonging to him, not to God and Christ (see comments on 2:13–14).

Given us understanding (5:20). Christians are not saved by "understanding" alone. But because salvation comes via Christ and the saving message that points to him, neither are Christians saved without "understanding." In contrast to this, another Jewish writer of the same era points to philosophical and speculative knowledge as what counts (see "Saving Understanding"). Plutarch likewise states that to live and die properly "we need a firm foundation based on reason and education."[87]

Eternal life (5:20). See comments on 2:25.

Keep yourselves from idols (5:21). Idols were a symbol of all that was wrong and evil in the pagan world; God had long ago condemned them through Moses in the second commandment (Ex. 20:4). Moreover, "the idea of making idols was the beginning of fornication, and the invention of them was the corruption of life" (Wisd. Sol. 14:12). People make them and use them because they "err about the knowledge of God" (14:22). John's readers are wonderfully spared the degrading fruit of false worship through the one who "is the true God and eternal life" (1 John 5:20).

ANNOTATED BIBLIOGRAPHY

Brown, Raymond. *The Epistles of John*. AB. Garden City, N.Y.: Doubleday, 1982.

Masterful and voluminous discussion of most background evidences and issues. Brown's stress on the polemical nature of 1 John may be overdone.

Burge, Gary. *The Epistles of John*. NIVAC. Grand Rapids: Zondervan, 1996.

Popular-level treatment with emphasis on application today.

Schlatter, Adolf. *The Theology of the Apostles*, trans. by Andreas Koestenberger. Grand Rapids: Baker, 1999, 108–85.

Insightful though not systematic treatment of the history and theology of John's letters.

Schnackenburg, Rudolf. *The Johannine Epistles*, trans. by Reginald and Ilse Fuller. New York: Crossroad, 1992.

In-depth analysis of the letters' message as well as their background. Good feel for elements of John's theology.

Strecker, Georg. *The Johannine Letters*, trans. by Linda M. Maloney, ed. by Harold Attridge. Philadelphia: Fortress, 1996.

Erudite rather than edifying. Reflects the critical, largely post-Christian outlook dominant in German universities. Notable as a barometer of late twentieth-century discussion. Valuable collection of background citations in footnotes.

Yarbrough, Robert. *1–3 John*. BECNT. Grand Rapids: Baker, forthcoming.

Pays close attention to the letters' grounding in the Old Testament and Jesus' teaching. Frequent allusions to Jewish, Greco-Roman, and patristic authors.

Main Text Notes

1. On Papias's date see R. Yarbrough, "The Date of Papias: A Reassessment," *JETS* 26 (1983): 181–91; Eusebius, *Eccl. Hist.* 3.39.17.
2. Eusebius, *Eccl. Hist.* 3.23.1.
3. Ephesus was by far the dominant city of the region. For information on its history and first-century status see L. F. DeVries, *Cities of the Biblical World* (Peabody, Mass.: Hendrickson, 1997), 372–79.
4. John evokes the memory of a famous Old Testament troublemaker; see 1 Kings 16:32–33; 18:4, 13; 19:1–2; 21.
5. John 14:15; 1 Thess. 1:3.
6. See, e.g., 1 John 1:6, 8, 10; 2:4, 6, 9, 11, 15, 24.
7. See Eusebius, *Eccl. Hist.* 3.27.
8. For a sample of a half dozen proposals see I. H. Marshall, *The Epistles of John* (Grand Rapids: Eerdmans, 1978), 22–27. Underscoring the unsatisfactory results of all outlines proposed thus far is Floyd V. Filson, "First John: Purpose and Message," *Int* 23 (1969): 261–63.
9. R. Schnackenburg, *The Johannine Epistles*, trans. Reginald and Ilse Fuller (New York: Crossroad, 1992), 12.
10. Denoted by small numerals in the inner margins of the modern Nestle-Aland Greek text.
11. Eusebius, *Eccl. Hist.*1.2.1.
12. Josephus, *Ant.* 4.8.15 §219.
13. Philo, *Moses* 1.4.
14. Josephus, *Ant.* 16.11.4 §376.
15. Josephus, *Life* 65 §§336–339; cf. Josephus' concern for fact in *Life* 65 §363–366.
16. Plutarch cited here and elsewhere from *Fall of the Roman Republic*, trans. Rex Warner (New York: Penguin, 1972).
17. *Exodus*, Book 2.
18. Georg Strecker, *The Johannine Letters*, trans. Linda M. Maloney, ed. Harold Attridge (Minneapolis: Fortress, 1996), 26. The similarities between Qumran thought and John are "concerns common to all great religions" (Thomas A. Hoffman, "1 John and the Qumran Scrolls," *BTB* 8 [1978]: 122) and do not necessitate an assumption of either literary dependence or direct social contact.
19. Everett Ferguson, *Backgrounds of Early Christianity* (Grand Rapids: Eerdmans, 1987), 222.
20. Ibid., 252–53.
21. Citing the translation by C. D. Yonge, *The Works of Philo* (Peabody, Mass.: Hendrickson, 1993); Philo, *Alleg. Interp.* 3.82.
22. E.g., 1 Kings 8:46; Prov. 20:9; Eccl. 7:20.
23. Philo, *Fragments* in Yonge, *The Works of Philo* 885.
24. Philo, *God* 75.
25. Ferguson, *Backgrounds of Early Christianity*, 118.
26. Ibid., 124.
27. Horace, *Odes* 3.6.
28. *The Community Rule* 8.21–23; 9.
29. Ignatius, *To the Smyrnaens* 6.
30. Ignatius, *To the Ephesians* 10.
31. Ibid., 7.
32. Ibid., 9.
33. Ibid., 53.
34. Finegan, *Myth and Mystery*, 166.
35. Xenophon, *Respublica Laccdaemoniorum* 10:8; Georg Strecker and Udo Schnelle, eds., *Neuer Wettstein* (Berlin/New York: Walter de Gruyter, 1996), 2:1429–30.
36. Ibid.
37. John J. Pilch and Bruce J. Malina, eds., *Handbook of Biblical Social Values* (Peabody, Mass.: Hendrickson, 1998), xxxii.
38. *Let. Aris.* 227–28.
39. John 8:44; 13:2; 1 John 3:8, 10; John 13:27; John 12:31; 14:30; 16:11.
40. My translation of a Philo fragment cited in Strecker and Schnelle, *Neuer Wettstein*, 2:1431.
41. Ibid., 2:1321.
42. Ibid., 2:1433; Porphyry, *De abstinentia* 1.54.3–4.
43. Ibid., 2:1432.
44. Philo, *Fragments* as translated by Yonge in *The Works of Philo* 890.
45. See John Anderson, "Cultural Assumptions Behind the First Epistle of John," *Notes on Translation* 4 (1990): 41.
46. *A Guide to the New Testament World* (Scottdale, Pa.: Herald, 1994), 149.
47. Moses Hadas, ed., *Essential Works of Stoicism* (New York: Bantam, 1961), 58.
48. Ibid., 88–89.
49. Polycarp, *Phil.* 7.
50. For discussion of "anointing" in ancient Jewish and Greek religion see Strecker, *The Johannine Letters*, 65–66.
51. Albert J. Bell Jr., *Exploring the New Testament World* (Nashville: Nelson, 1998), 172.
52. For stinging rejection of the notion of hope, see Plutarch, *Fall of the Roman Republic*, *Gaius Marius* 46.
53. E.g., 4:1, 9, 10, 40; 5:16, 33; 8:1, 3; 11:9; 12:1, 10; 16:20; 17:19; 25:15; 30:15, 16, 19, 20; 32:39, 47.
54. Josephus, *Life* 65 §366.

55. Tertullian, *Apology* 9.
56. 1 John 4:15; 5:5, 10, 12, 13, 20.
57. 1 John 1:3, 7; 2:22, 23, 24; 3:23; 4:9, 10, 14; 5:9, 10, 20; 2 John 3, 9.
58. Suetonius, *Caesars* 94.
59. Seneca, *Ep.* 72.6.
60. Ibid., 120.10; Strecker and Schnelle, *Neuer Wettstein*, 2:1435–36.
61. Dio Chrysostom, *Orations* 4.21–23.
62. Ibid., 2:1437.
63. Philo, QG 1.59–60.
64. Josephus, *Ant.* 1.2.1 §54.
65. Ibid., 1.2.2 §61; see "Josephus on Cain."
66. Hadas, ed., *Essential Works of Stoicism*, 77.
67. Stephen M. Wylen, *The Jews in the Time of Jesus* (New York/Mahwah, N.J.: Paulist, 1996), 92.
68. J. M. Court, "Blessed Assurance?" *JTS* 33 (1982): 508–17.
69. Markus Bockmühl, *Revelation and Mystery in Ancient Judaism and Pauline Christianity* (WUNT 2/36; Tübingen: J. C. B. Mohr [Paul Siebeck], 1990), 20.
70. Plutarch, *Fall of the Roman Republic, Gaius Marius* 17.
71. Philo, *Spec. Laws* 1.315; Josephus, *J.W.* 6.5.2 §§285–88.
72. Walter A. Elwell, ed., *Topical Analysis of the Bible* (Grand Rapids: Baker, 1991), 24–34.
73. Seneca, *On Providence* 5.8–9.
74. Philo, *Contempl. Life* 90, Yonge trans..
75. Wisd. Sol. 7:28; cf. Sir. 4:14.
76. See, e.g., 2 Kings 17:14, 40; 2 Chron. 24:19; Ps. 81:11; Isa. 28:12; Jer. 6:17; Zech. 7:12.
77. *1 En.* 62:10.
78. Strecker and Schnelle, *Neuer Wettstein*, 2:1439; Cicero, *De Officiis* 2.23–24.
79. Ibid.
80. John T. McNeill, ed., *Calvin: Institutes of the Christian Religion*, trans. Ford Lewis Battles (Philadelphia: Westminster, 1960), 1:40.
81. Philo, *Decalogue* 120, Yonge trans.
82. Strecker and Schnelle, *Neuer Wettstein*, 2:1440; Plutarch, *Moralia* 480 d–f.
83. Josephus, *Ag. Ap.* 1.8 §46.
84. Philo, *Posterity* 128–29.
85. Ferguson, *Backgrounds of Early Christianity*, 149–50.
86. Conveniently accessible in Herbert Lockyer, *All the Prayers of the Bible* (Grand Rapids: Zondervan, 1979).
87. *Fall of the Roman Republic, Gaius Marius* 46.

Sidebar and Chart Notes

A-1. W. H. C. Frend, *Martyrdom and Persecution in the Early Church* (Grand Rapids: Baker, 1981), 213.
A-2. Cerinthus, *Against Heresies* 1.26.1.
A-3. Philo, *Providence* Fragment 2.53, Yonge translation, 754.
A-4. Jack Finegan, *Myth and Mystery* (Grand Rapids: Baker, 1989), 166.
A-5. Philo, *Moses* 1.30–31, Yonge translation.
A-6. *Community Rule* 1, cited here and below according to Geza Vermes, ed., *The Dead Sea Scrolls in English* (New York: Penguin, 1985), 72.
A-7. *Community Rule* IV, Vermes, *Dead Sea Scrolls*, 77.
A-8. Cited according to Geza Vermes, ed., *The Dead Sea Scrolls in English* (New York: Penguin, 1985), 251–52.
A-9. *The Manual* 16, in Moses Hadas, ed., *Essential Works of Stoicism* (New York: Bantam, 1961), 89.
A-10. Kenneth McLeish, ed., *Key Ideas in Human Thought* (Rocklin, Calif.: Prima, 1995), 681.
A-11. *Manual* 9.
A-12. Ibid., 1.2.2 §66, Whiston translation.
A-13. Ibid., 6.6, 7, 9.
A-14. *Odes Sol.* 41:1–6.
A-15. Philo, *Cherubim* 2, 48.
A-16. Ibid., 2, 43–44, Yonge translation.

2 JOHN

by Robert Yarbrough

The Setting of 2 John

Little is known outside of what the letter itself contains. Because the language and topics of 2 John are similar to those found in 1 John, and since both letters appear to have the same author, it is reasonable to conclude that they are addressing similar concerns. These include obeying what "the Father commanded" (4), resisting heresy (7–8), and contributing to the Christian joy that the apostolic message brings to the world by continuing an authentic embrace of the gospel (12).

For reflections on the possible setting, see "The Setting of 1 John" in the introduction to 1 John.

Structure of the Letter

The organization reflects the conventions of a Hellenistic letter:

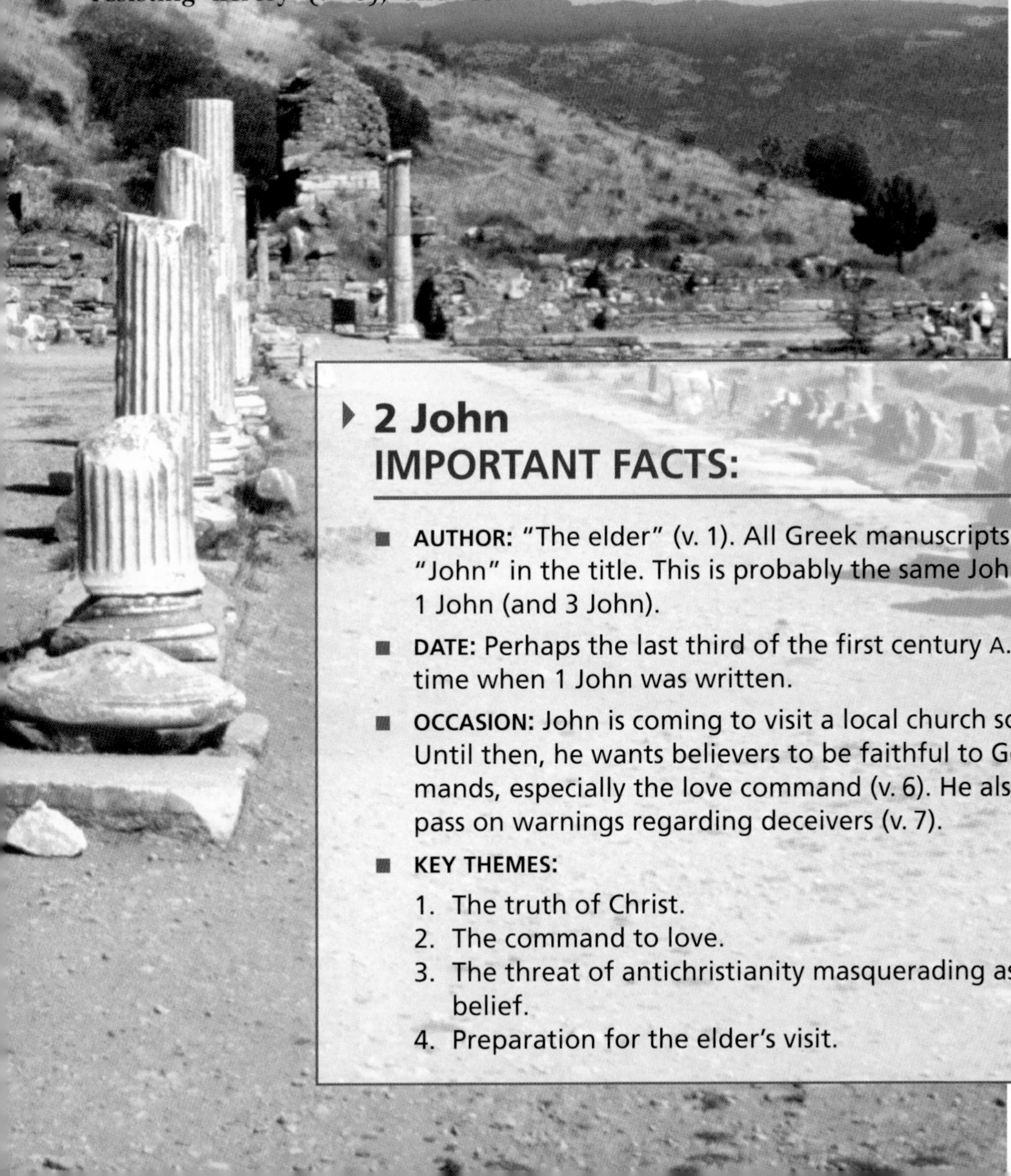

EPHESUS

The remains of the first-century A.D. Basilica of Augustus.

◀

▸ 2 John IMPORTANT FACTS:

- **AUTHOR:** "The elder" (v. 1). All Greek manuscripts name "John" in the title. This is probably the same John who wrote 1 John (and 3 John).
- **DATE:** Perhaps the last third of the first century A.D., near the time when 1 John was written.
- **OCCASION:** John is coming to visit a local church soon (v. 12). Until then, he wants believers to be faithful to God's commands, especially the love command (v. 6). He also needs to pass on warnings regarding deceivers (v. 7).
- **KEY THEMES:**
  1. The truth of Christ.
  2. The command to love.
  3. The threat of antichristianity masquerading as gospel belief.
  4. Preparation for the elder's visit.

author's name and greetings (1–3), body of letter (4–11), final words and farewell (12–13). What is different from a Hellenistic letter is the content of each section. John expresses thoughts, concerns, and convictions (e.g., "Grace, mercy and peace from God the Father and from Jesus Christ," v. 3) that are foreign to normal Greco-Roman correspondence. (For samples of ancient letters see "Ancient Letters"' in the introduction to 3 John.)

Message of the Letter

The letter serves as a stopgap until a longer, personal visit is possible (v. 12). The writer assumes much more information than he actually conveys. But what he does convey may be summarized by taking note of the letter's commands:

- v. 5: love one another
- v. 8: watch out lest you lose your reward
- v. 10: do not support the travels and ministry of heretical Christian leaders
- v. 12: be prepared for an apostolic visit

Assumptions of the Letter

Among ancient churches 2 John seems to have struggled to find universal acceptance. But its underlying premises are consistent with apostolic Christianity as modeled in other New Testament letters. These premises include:

- the close identification of the true and living God with Jesus Christ his Son (3)
- the validity and redemptive power of the commands coming from this God (4–6)
- the importance of right belief concerning God's Son (7)
- the promise of heavenly reward, assuming believers' faithful perseverance (8)
- the responsibility of Christians to participate in the furthering of Christ's kingdom through (discerning) support of gospel messengers (10–11)
- the joy of knowing God in Christ (12)
- the communion of saints in churches everywhere (1, 13)

The elder (1). In early Christianity "elders" were the leaders or shepherds of local congregations—in other words, they were pastors.[1] But an apostle could also refer to himself as an elder, as Peter does: "To the elders among you, I appeal as a fellow elder" (1 Peter 5:1). In other words, the word "elder" could apply to an apostle and thus to the "elder" John, the apostle—especially in his pastoral capacity among Asia Minor congregations.[2] The apostles did not see themselves as social superiors to elders but as their coworkers in the gospel and as "brothers" to other Christians of all levels (Acts 15:23).

The chosen lady (1). The word translated "lady" is the Greek word *kyria*. Some have thought that John refers to a female person by the name Kyria or to an anonymous "select lady." But this Greek word was also used for a sociopolitical subdivision in Athens, a subdivision of the larger *ekklesia* (often translated in the New Testament as "church").[3] John appears to be using a word for a local congregation that is not attested elsewhere in early Christian writings. This word is chosen because of distinctive local social and linguistic conventions about which we have no additional information. "Chosen lady," then, simply means a local congregation who, as God's people, are by definition "elect" or "chosen" (a common term for Christians; see, e.g., Rom. 16:13; 1 Peter 1:1; 2:9).

All who know the truth (1; cf. 2, 3, 4). Among pagan writers "truth" was arrived at by rational contemplation or by observation of nature, or perhaps by both. There was no widespread agreement on what truth is, on how knowledge of it can be assured, or on what, if anything, ought to be done once truth has been determined.

For biblical writers there is a common conviction that truth relates closely to God; he is "the God of truth" (Ps. 31:5; cf. Isa. 65:16). Truth is God's possession. It is grounded in his nature just as love is (Ps. 40:11). God sends forth truth like light; this truth guides us to the place where God dwells (43:3). God's truth will be the basis for final judgment: "He will judge the world in righteousness and the peoples in his truth" (96:13). God always speaks the truth: "I, the LORD, speak the truth; I declare what is right" (Isa. 45:19). God commands his people to seek and love truth (Jer. 5:3; Zech. 8:16, 19). Truth is not rational knowledge alone but relates equally to "wisdom, discipline and understanding" (Prov. 23:23). Truth is found in God's word (Ps. 119:30).

Jesus claimed to speak the truth he had heard from God (John 8:40). He claimed to be "the truth" that leads to God (14:6) and equated truth with God's word (17:17). He told Pilate that he "came into the world, to testify to the truth," and added, "Everyone on the side of truth listens to me" (18:37).

Jesus' apostles saw truth as residing in Christ and the gospel message about him (Gal. 2:5, 14; Col. 1:5). Christians are "taught in [Christ] in accordance with the truth that is in Jesus" (Eph. 4:21). Truth is part of the Christian's armor: "Stand firm then, with the belt of truth buckled around your waist" (6:14). To reject the truth of the gospel is to be eternally lost (2 Thess. 2:12). Truth is not something merely known but is to be sought and loved (2:10). Belief in the truth is the way to be saved (2:13). The church is "the pillar and foundation of the truth" (1 Tim. 3:15). Gospel truth "leads to godliness" (Titus 1:1); it is not about abstract speculation but an honest and godly life. Obeying God's truth leads to love for others (1 Peter 1:22).

The Johannine letters contain numerous references to "truth."[4] No single definition explains every occurrence. The references seem to fit into the following categories:

(1) Truth is possessed and imparted by the Holy Spirit, who is truth.[5]

◀ *left*

CHOSEN LADY

Painted statue of a woman from Amphipolis.

(2) Truth refers to the ethical standards God has established for his people as expressed in his commandments.[6]
(3) Truth is God's sanctifying presence, which gives the believer the capacity to reflect God's character traits, such as love and aversion to sin.[7]
(4) Truth refers to the quality of conformity to the way things are in God's omniscient wisdom (2:8).
(5) Truth refers to the gospel of Jesus Christ, its implications, and the sphere of eternal life into which the gospel ushers those who embrace it.[8]

A famous ancient tale praises truth as the greatest of all powers on earth (see "The Greatness of Truth"). But "truth" in this story, while it may be defined as the expression and outworking of the perfect divine will, lacks the personal and living dimension of "truth" as portrayed in Scripture. Nor is truth primarily just a matter of not telling lies (as implied in *Let. Aris.* 206).

The Johannine letters are distinct in their clear, forceful, and diverse characterization of God—Father, Son, and Holy Spirit—as the God of truth. This truth is known particularly through the gospel and is mediated to believers by the Spirit. The test of truth is not intellectual brilliance or scientific accuracy (though these are not disparaged) but divinely imparted character traits, especially love and compassion for others and zeal for Christ's gospel and ways.

Great joy (4). For Stoic thinkers joy, like all strong emotions, was to be avoided. But joy had always accompanied news of Jesus: There was joy at his birth (Luke 1:14; 2:10); there was joy among his disciples as they ministered (10:17); there was joy in the presence of the Lord after his resurrection (24:41, 52). Jesus had promised abundant joy to his disciples (see John 15:11; 16:20, 24). Jesus prayed to the Father that his followers would have joy after he left them (17:13).

Joy is often associated with human celebration, but this is too simplistic: "Even in laughter the heart may ache,

The Greatness of Truth

A Hellenistic understanding of truth is dramatized by the famous story of three youths who sought their king's approval by staging a debate to settle which is strongest: wine, the king, or women. The winner of the contest argued, "Women are strongest, but truth is victor over all things" (1 Esd. 3:12). To truth is ascribed "the power and majesty of the ages." In the Johannine letters, truth describes qualities of God's being, his work, and his revelation, but it is never receives the praise that belongs to God alone. In the story, the winning debater argues as follows (4:35–36, 38–40):

Truth is great, and stronger than all things. The whole earth calls upon truth, and heaven blesses it.... Truth endures and is strong forever, and lives and prevails forever and ever. With it there is no partiality or preference, but it does what is righteous instead of anything that is unrighteous or wicked.... To it belongs the strength and the kingship and the power and the majesty of all the ages. Blessed be the God of truth!

and joy may end in grief" (Prov. 14:13). True joy comes from participation in the kingdom of God, which is not a matter of partying, "of eating and drinking, but of righteousness, peace and joy in the Holy Spirit" (Rom. 14:17). Joy is a fruit of the Holy Spirit (Gal. 5:22).

The joy John expresses is closely related to the love he has for his readers. Shared labor for Christ's sake brings a sense of togetherness, appreciation for each other, and praise for the Lord because he forgives our sins and is redeeming our lives. Such work together often involves fervent prayer, sacrifice, and even suffering; these are powerful bonding agents in human relationships, especially when they are truly for Christ's sake. The result can be a profound shared sense of how great the message of the cross is and what a privilege it is to share in gospel ministry, benefits, and challenges. This is to say nothing of the indescribable joy of the presence of Christ himself through his Spirit. This is most likely the sort of joy of which John speaks.

Dear lady (5). John probably addresses the congregation as a whole; see comments on verse 1.

Not . . . a new command (5). See comments on 1 John 2:7 and 2:8.

From the beginning (5–6). See comments on 1 John 1:1.

This is love: that we walk in obedience to his commands (6). See comments on 1 John 5:3. Some religions seem obsessed with commands; Paul may have been addressing such a viewpoint in Colossians 2:20–23. Other religious perspectives seem intent on rejecting or flaunting the commands of Scripture (Titus 1:16; 2 Peter 2). Jesus warned of a time when disregard for God's law would be widespread (Matt. 24:12). John apparently feels the necessity of stressing that those who claim to know and love God must be diligent in seeking to obey Christ's commands and follow his example. This is exactly what Jesus taught during the last hours of his life on this earth.[9]

Deceivers (7). See comments on 1 John 3:7; 4:1; see also "Challenges Confronting the Churches" in the introduction to 1 John. Some scholars think that the warning against docetic doctrine in 1 John 4:2 is different from the warning in 2 John 7. In the 1 John passage the word translated "has come" is in the perfect tense. But in 2 John 7 the word translated "coming" is in the present tense. Accordingly, in 2 John the warning is perhaps against those who deny the "coming" appearance of Christ on earth, that is, his literal physical return in judgment and glory to inaugurate an earthly messianic era.

The antichrist (7). See comments on 1 John 2:18.

ANTISTHENES

This philosopher (445–360 B.C.) was a follower of Socrates and a major influence on the development of Cynicism.

ATHLETE WITH WREATHS

A stone relief from Isthmia depicting a victorious athlete with his crowns.

Runs ahead (9). This unusual expression is probably explained by what follows: "does not continue in the teaching of Christ." While apostolic Christianity was richly creative, it was equally committed to a definite and sure foundation (see comments on 1 John 1:1). This means that sheer novelty was unwelcome if it was felt to be untrue and therefore destructive of the gospel message, which could not be tampered with (cf. Gal. 1:8–9; Jude 3).

Do not take him into your house (10). This is not a contradiction of Christian teaching elsewhere that commends hospitality to strangers (e.g., Heb. 13:2). False teachers are no longer strangers once their identity becomes public knowledge! John has in mind the kind of hospitality that Jesus told his followers to look for in Luke 10:5–8. To open one's home to non- or quasi-Christian religious propagandists for the sake of their ministry is forbidden to Christians. An ancient Greek father warned his son, "The evil man wants the good man to turn bad so he will become like him."[10]

John's warning in no way questions philanthropic work by Christians on behalf of non-Christians—rescue missions, building projects, prison ministries, care for the homeless, medical missions, educational initiatives, disaster relief, and other outreaches too numerous to detail. It may call in question, however, the tendency of some in recent times to put the resources of Christian churches at the disposal of "interfaith" enterprises whose main effect seems to be the dethronement of Jesus Christ from his place as sole Lord and Savior and the replacement of evangelical Christianity with a "tolerant" humanitarianism bearing only negative resemblance to the gospel of Christ's death and resurrection (see also comments on 3 John 8).

Joy (12). See comments on verse 4.

Chosen sister (13). Since the author of 2 John refers to the congregation he addresses as "chosen lady [*kyria*]" in verse 1, he may be extending the metaphor in verse 13 in referring to a "sister" congregation, using language of the nuclear family.

ANNOTATED BIBLIOGRAPHY

Brown, Raymond. *The Epistles of John.* AB. Garden City, N.Y.: Doubleday, 1982.
Masterful and voluminous discussion of most background evidences and issues. Brown's stress on the polemical nature of 1 John may be overdone.

Burge, Gary. *The Epistles of John.* NIVAC. Grand Rapids: Zondervan, 1996.
Popular-level treatment with emphasis on application today.

Schlatter, Adolf. *The Theology of the Apostles,* trans. by Andreas Koestenberger. Grand Rapids: Baker, 1999, 108–85.
Insightful though not systematic treatment of the history and theology of John's letters.

Schnackenburg, Rudolf. *The Johannine Epistles,* trans. by Reginald and Ilse Fuller. New York: Crossroad, 1992.
In-depth analysis of the letters' message as well as their background. Good feel for elements of John's theology.

Strecker, Georg. *The Johannine Letters,* trans. by Linda M. Maloney, ed. by Harold Attridge. Philadelphia: Fortress, 1996.
Erudite rather than edifying. Reflects the critical, largely post-Christian outlook dominant in German universities. Notable as a barometer of late twentieth-century discussion. Valuable collection of background citations in footnotes.

Yarbrough, Robert. *1–3 John.* BECNT. Grand Rapids: Baker, forthcoming.
Pays close attention to the letters' grounding in the Old Testament and Jesus' teaching. Frequent allusions to Jewish, Greco-Roman, and patristic authors.

CHAPTER NOTES

Main Text Notes

1. Acts 14:23; 15:2, 4, 6, 22, 23; 16:4; 20:17; 21:18; 1 Tim. 5:17, 19; Titus 1:5; James 5:14.
2. Eusebius, *Eccl. Hist.* 3.23.1.
3. Strecker and Schnelle, *Neuer Wettstein,* 2:1442.
4. 1 John 1:6, 8; 2:4, 8, 20, 21; 3:18, 19; 4:6; 5:6; 2 John 1, 2, 3, 4; 3 John 1, 3, 4, 8, 12.
5. 1 John 2:20; 4:6; 5:6; 3 John 12.
6. 1 John 1:6; 2:21; 3:18; 2 John 4; 3 John 3, 4.
7. 1 John 1:8; 2:4, 21.
8. 1 John 3:19; 2 John 1, 2, 3; 3 John 1, 8.
9. John 13:17; 14:21, 23–24; 15:9, 10–12, 14, 17.
10. Strecker and Schnelle, *Neuer Wettstein,* 2:1443.

3 JOHN

by Robert Yarbrough

The Setting of 3 John

Like 2 John, there are few definite clues to a historical setting outside of what 3 John itself contains—and these are vague. Because the language of 3 John is so similar to that of 2 John and since both appear to share a common author, the setting of these little letters may be closely related. Words that both letters share include "truth," "children," and "love." Both speak of those who "went out" (v. 7), although in 3 John this is a positive movement while in 2 John it refers to the spread of false teaching. Both letters speak of the imminent coming of the writer, who calls himself "the elder." This elder rejoices that his readers "walk in the truth" in both letters. Some even feel that the letter referred to in 3 John 9 ("I wrote to the church") is 2 John.[1]

COUNTRYSIDE AROUND EPHESUS

This is near the traditional site of the prison of St. Paul.

3 John IMPORTANT FACTS:

- **AUTHOR:** "The elder" (v. 1). All Greek manuscripts name "John" in the title. This is probably the same John who wrote 1 John (and 2 John, judging from numerous close similarities of language).
- **DATE:** Perhaps the last third of the first century A.D., close to when 2 John was written.
- **OCCASION:** John will soon be visiting his dear friend Gaius (1, 14). Until then, he wishes Gaius well (2), commends his faithfulness (5), warns him regarding a troublemaker (9), exhorts him to do good (11), commends Demetrius (the letter carrier?), and promises a speedy arrival (14).
- **KEY THEMES:**
  1. The shared joy of perseverance in Christian faith.
  2. The importance of Christian hospitality.
  3. The existence of church division.
  4. The importance of ethics to legitimate Christian confession.

For broader reflections on the possible setting of the author, assuming that John wrote all three letters that bear his name, see "The Setting of 1 John" in the introduction to 1 John.

Structure of the Letter

Like 2 John, 3 John's organization reflects the conventions of a Hellenistic letter: author's name (or title) and greetings (1), prayer for and commendation of the reader (2–4), body of letter (5–12), and final words and farewell (13–14). One scholar notes, "Third John very much resembles a common papyrus letter as the writer commends certain travelers and censures a certain Diotrephes"[2] (see "Ancient Letters").

Message of the Letter

"The elder" plans to arrive soon (14). This short letter serves to:

- express the joy that the author shares with Gaius (3–4)

▸ Ancient Letters

Short notes to friends and family did not begin with the invention of e-mail. Even in New Testament times people sent letters. Some of these letters, written on papyrus and dug up from the desert sands of Egypt, have features like those found in 2 and 3 John.

This letter from about A.D. 25 (Oxy. 292[A-1]) predates any possible Christian influence. But the length, organization, and certain concerns (commendation of a joint acquaintance, wishes for health) resemble similar features in 2 or 3 John.

> Theon to his esteemed Tyrannos, many greetings. Herakleides, the bearer of this letter, is my brother. I therefore entreat you with all my power to treat him as your protégé. I have also written to your brother Hermias, asking him to communicate with you about him. You will confer upon me a very great favor if Herakleides gains your notice. Before all else you have my good wishes for unbroken health and prosperity. Good-bye.

A second example[A-2] (third century A.D.) does show Christian influence. Like 3 John it mentions God, truth, and the reader's health and soul. "Comforter" is John's term for the Holy Spirit in the Fourth Gospel. A Christian boy named Besas writes to his mother:

> To my most precious mother, from Besas, many greetings in God. Before all I pray to our Father, the God of truth, and to the Spirit who is the Comforter that he may guard you in soul, body, and spirit, and give health to your body, cheerfulness to your spirit, and eternal life to your soul. If you find someone coming my direction, do not hesitate to write me a letter concerning your health so that I might hear and rejoice. Do not neglect to send my cloak for the Easter holiday and send my brother to me. I salute my father and my brothers. I pray that all of you might have continual good health.

- commend Gaius and his church for the support of itinerant missionaries (5–8)
- mention a problem that his arisen with a certain Diotrephes (9–10)
- convey advice, personal information, and the promise to visit soon (11–14)

A social-science reading interprets 3 John as a formal letter of recommendation.[3] In this view the letter should be understood primarily as a reflection of first-century Mediterranean social posturing: "The elder" has been challenged by Diotrephes, so "the elder" sends Demetrius, with a letter of commendation, to Gaius. Gaius (and others who receive John's words favorably) then becomes an ally for "the elder" in advance of his coming visit to put Diotrephes in his place. The letter is therefore not strictly private. It has a private addressee, Gaius, but is intended to serve a somewhat public function—the function of reestablishing the honor of "the elder" after Diotrephes has disparaged it.

The advantage of the social-science approach is that it brings important insights and considerations (like the values of honor and shame in that culture) to the discussion of 3 John's interpretation. Its drawback is that it may tend to reduce 3 John to no more than the sum total of social interrelations. However important honor and shame may have been for named players in the social drama, the transcendent realities denoted by the letter's language (truth, God, the Name, the church, good, evil, testimony, peace) should retain their central importance. Also, as an apostle who had seen and lived with the Lord (1 John 1:1–4), John's written counsel would not only relate to, but also tower above, the social categories of first-century Mediterranean culture, at least for those who received the gospel as the unique saving message of eternal life.

Features of the Letter

Like 2 John, 3 John seems to have struggled to find universal acceptance among ancient churches. But its content and tone are consistent with apostolic Christianity as modeled in other New Testament letters. Among distinctly Christian features are:

- John's and Gaius's mutual affection in the truth (of the gospel of Jesus Christ) (1–3; cf. 14, reciprocal greetings of "friends")
- the priority of Christian outreach for the whole church and of the support of those who go forth "for the sake of the Name" (5–8)
- a frank acknowledgment of tensions among early Christian leaders (9–10)
- the importance of good behavior as an expression of embracing true doctrine (11)

The elder (1). See comments on 2 John 1.

Love in the truth (1; cf. "truth" at 3, 4, 8, 12). The elder has a love for Gaius, a shared "group attraction and group bonding,"[4] because of their common life in the gospel of Jesus Christ. On "truth" see comments on 2 John 1.

Good health (2). Wishes for good health were typical in letter greetings, much like casual references to the weather in a modern English letter. But the wish could also be sincere. Life expectancy was half that of modern Western standards, and for most sickness and disease there was no sure cure. Seneca (*On the Shortness of Life* 1.1) voiced a common first-century perception that "the space that has been granted to us rushes by so speedily and so swiftly that all save a very few find life at an end just when they are getting ready to live." Antibiotics and effective medication for pain did not exist. Death could snatch away a loved one, or oneself, with little warning. So it is understandable that wishes for good health echo frequently in epistolary greetings.

What about the healing power of the gospel? Even though miraculous healings did take place in the early church, they were exceptional. Even an apostle like Paul could not perform them at will (1 Tim. 5:23; 2 Tim. 4:20). Sometimes physical ailments are God's will for his servants (2 Cor. 12:7–10).

Joy (4). See comments on 2 John 4.

Walking in the truth (4). See also "love in the truth" (1) and comments on "truth" at 2 John 1. To walk in the truth means to live in the light of the gospel. It also involves honoring God's commands (see comments on 2 John 6). "Walking in the truth" is an expression that probably seemed natural to early Christians because of Old Testament phraseology.[5] In places this wording is retained in a modern translation like the NIV (Ps. 26:3; 86:11).

Your love (6). Gaius's love is not an emotional sensation but a concrete act of compassion on behalf of traveling Christians, probably missionaries, whom Gaius did not even know. Love here relates closely to obedience to God's commands regarding how to treat others (see comments on 1 John 2:5, 7, 8, 11, 18; 4:8, 11).

Send them on their way (6). The Greek verb used here (*propempō*) often connotes sending forth with necessary resources.[6] Churches were expected to support Christian missionaries and other Christian workers, financially and other-

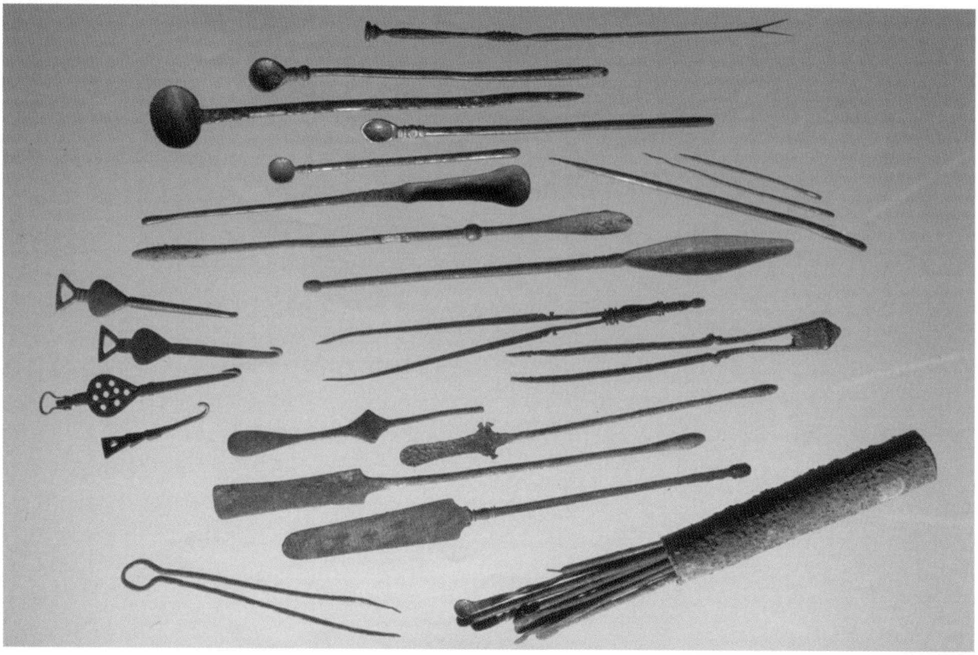

TOOLS OF A ROMAN DOCTOR

wise, as they carried out their ministries. This is most evident in Paul's words to Titus: "Do everything you can to help Zenas the lawyer and Apollos on their way and see that they have everything they need" (Titus 3:13). James warns against phony hospitality, the verbal blessing masking material stinginess (James 2:15–16).

Show hospitality (8). Opening one's home to other Christians, even if they were strangers (5), was important for the survival and spread of the gospel.[7] Inns were not found everywhere, and conditions in them could be marginal.[8] Often "sleeping quarters were filthy and insect and rodent infested, inn-keepers were extortionate, thieves were in wait, government spies were listening, and many [inns] were nothing more than brothels."[9]

The demands and risks of showing hospitality are acknowledged in a pre-Christian Jewish document that found its way into the Bible of many early churches because it was included in the Greek version of the Old Testament (see "Warning Against Showing Hospitality").

Loves to be first (9). Seneca noted that "no man is able to rule unless he can also submit to be ruled."[10] Apparently Diotrephes enjoyed wielding power but had little desire to defer to someone else's judgment. Among Jesus' followers highest honor is not supposed to attach to power but to humility and servanthood (Matt. 18:3; 23:11). His disciples argued more than once about who was greatest, right under the nose of their master (Luke 9:46; 22:24). It is therefore no wonder that in later generations of the church the problem crops up regularly.

Will have nothing to do with us (9). The same word is translated "refuses to welcome" in verse 10.[11]

SHOW HOSPITALITY

Modern Samaritan men seated around a table at mealtime.

Warning Against Showing Hospitality

While "the elder" commends an open-door policy toward traveling Christian workers, Sirach warns against receiving strangers into one's home (Sir. 11:29–34):

> Do not invite everyone into your home,
> for many are the tricks of the crafty.
> Like a decoy partridge in a cage, so is the mind of the proud,
> and like spies they observe your weakness;
> for they lie in wait, turning good into evil,
> and to worthy actions they attach blame.
> From a spark many coals are kindled,
> and a sinner lies in wait to shed blood.
> Beware of scoundrels, for they devise evil,
> and may ruin your reputation forever.
> Receive strangers into your home and they will stir up trouble for you,
> and will make you a stranger to your own family.

Imitate . . . what is good (11). Gaius should not imitate the bad example of Diotrephes. He should rather respond to the capacity for love and the pursuit of God's goodness that the gospel makes possible. That is what "walking in the truth" (4) is all about. Different is a pagan writer's advice on how to subdue evil in the heart: "Yet nothing is so hard and difficult that it cannot be conquered by the human intellect and be brought through persistent study into intimate acquaintance, and there are no passions so fierce and self-willed that they cannot be subjugated by self-discipline."[12] John teaches we should look to Jesus Christ for salvation from evil, not to human reason and self-discipline.

Our testimony is true (12). See comments on 1 John 1:1. John refers to the apostolic eyewitness, not the generic testimony of Christian belief alone.

Peace to you (14). Philo is credited with writing, "Peace is the greatest blessing, which no man is able to afford, since this is a divine action."[13] "Peace" was the greeting of the risen Jesus Christ to John and the other disciples (John 20:19, 21, 26). As an apostle John passes on that greeting to other believers with particular assurance. With that same word "peace" Christians have greeted one another through the centuries.

REFLECTIONS

THE APOSTLE JOHN RECOGNIZES a sworn enemy of the gospel in Diotrephes. What was he up to that was so wrong?

The problem was apparently not a "big" sin like murder or flagrant moral lapse. It was rather a combination of "little" problems—some of them seemingly harmless. Diotrephes "loves to be first." Don't we all? And then he gossips some. It's pretty hard not to talk about people at all. And then he "refuses to welcome the brothers" and shows the door to people who disagree with his character judgments. Maybe he was zealous for the purity of the church. Isn't "purity" one of John's own concerns (1 John 3:3)? As for his defiance of John's leadership—didn't John teach that "perfect love drives out fear" (4:18)? Maybe Diotrephes was just exercising the bold confidence he inferred from John's pastoral teaching.

It is easy to make excuses for sub-Christian attitudes and behavior. But when what we say or do goes against apostolic counsel—which for us means Holy Scripture—we are near the edge of a precipice. It doesn't take many "little" willful missteps to move us a great distance from the mercy and grace of Christ.

ANNOTATED BIBLIOGRAPHY

Brown, Raymond. *The Epistles of John.* AB. Garden City, N.Y.: Doubleday, 1982.
Masterful and voluminous discussion of most background evidences and issues. Brown's stress on the polemical nature of 1 John may be overdone.

Burge, Gary. *The Epistles of John.* NIVAC. Grand Rapids: Zondervan, 1996.
Popular-level treatment with emphasis on application today.

Schlatter, Adolf. *The Theology of the Apostles,* trans. by Andreas Koestenberger. Grand Rapids: Baker, 1999, 108–85.
Insightful though not systematic treatment of the history and theology of John's letters.

Schnackenburg, Rudolf. *The Johannine Epistles,* trans. by Reginald and Ilse Fuller. New York: Crossroad, 1992.
In-depth analysis of the letters' message as well as their background. Good feel for elements of John's theology.

Strecker, Georg. *The Johannine Letters,* trans. by Linda M. Maloney, ed. by Harold Attridge. Philadelphia: Fortress, 1996.
Erudite rather than edifying. Reflects the critical, largely post-Christian outlook dominant in German universities. Notable as a barometer of late twentieth-century discussion. Valuable collection of background citations in footnotes.

Yarbrough, Robert. *1–3 John.* BECNT. Grand Rapids: Baker, forthcoming.
Pays close attention to the letters' grounding in the Old Testament and Jesus' teaching. Frequent allusions to Jewish, Greco-Roman, and patristic authors.

CHAPTER NOTES

Main Text Notes

1. Strecker, *The Johannine Letters,* 253–54.
2. Stanley K. Stowers, *Letter Writing in Greco-Roman Antiquity* (Philadelphia: Westminster, 1986), 43.
3. Bruce J. Malina, "The Received View and What It Cannot Do: III John and Hospitality," *Semeia* 35 (1986): 171–94.
4. John J. Pilch and Bruce J. Malina, eds., *Handbook of Biblical Social Values* (Peabody, Mass.: Hendrickson, 1998), 127.
5. 1 Kings 2:4; 3:14; 2 Kings 20:3; Isa. 38:3.
6. Acts 15:3; Rom. 15:24; 1 Cor. 16:6, 11; 2 Cor. 1:16.
7. See Rom. 16:23; Heb. 13:2; 1 Peter 4:9; 2 John 10.
8. Abraham J. Malherbe, *Social Aspects of Early Christianity,* 2d ed. (Philadelphia: Fortress, 1985), 95.
9. Ferguson, *Backgrounds of Early Christianity,* 67.
10. Seneca, *On Anger* 2.15.4.
11. For discussion see Margaret M. Mitchell, "'Diotrephes Does Not Receive Us': The Lexicographical and Social Context of 3 John 9–10," *JBL* 117 (Summer 1998): 299–320.
12. Seneca, *On Anger* 2.12.3.
13. *Fragments Preserved by Antonius,* Ser. 56; Cited from Yonge, *The Works of Philo* 893.

Sidebar and Chart Notes

A-1. Adapted slightly from Adolf Deissmann, *Bible Studies,* trans. Alexander Grieve (Edinburgh: T. & T. Clark, 1901), 23.

A-2. Stowers, *Letter Writing in Greco-Roman Antiquity,* 74.

JUDE

by Douglas J. Moo

Jude

Most English translations use the name "Jude" only here in the New Testament. In fact, however, the Greek behind "Jude" is *Ioudas*, a name that occurs forty-three other times in the New Testament. It is usually translated "Judah," referring to the Old Testament patriarch or the territory within Israel named after him, or "Judas." The latter, of course, usually refers to Judas Iscariot, the betrayer of Jesus. But the name is also given to four other men who appear in the New Testament: (1) "Judas the Galilean," a revolutionary; (2) "Judas son of James," one of the Twelve; (3) "Judas, called Barsabbas," an early Christian prophet; and (4) a brother of Jesus named "Judas."[1]

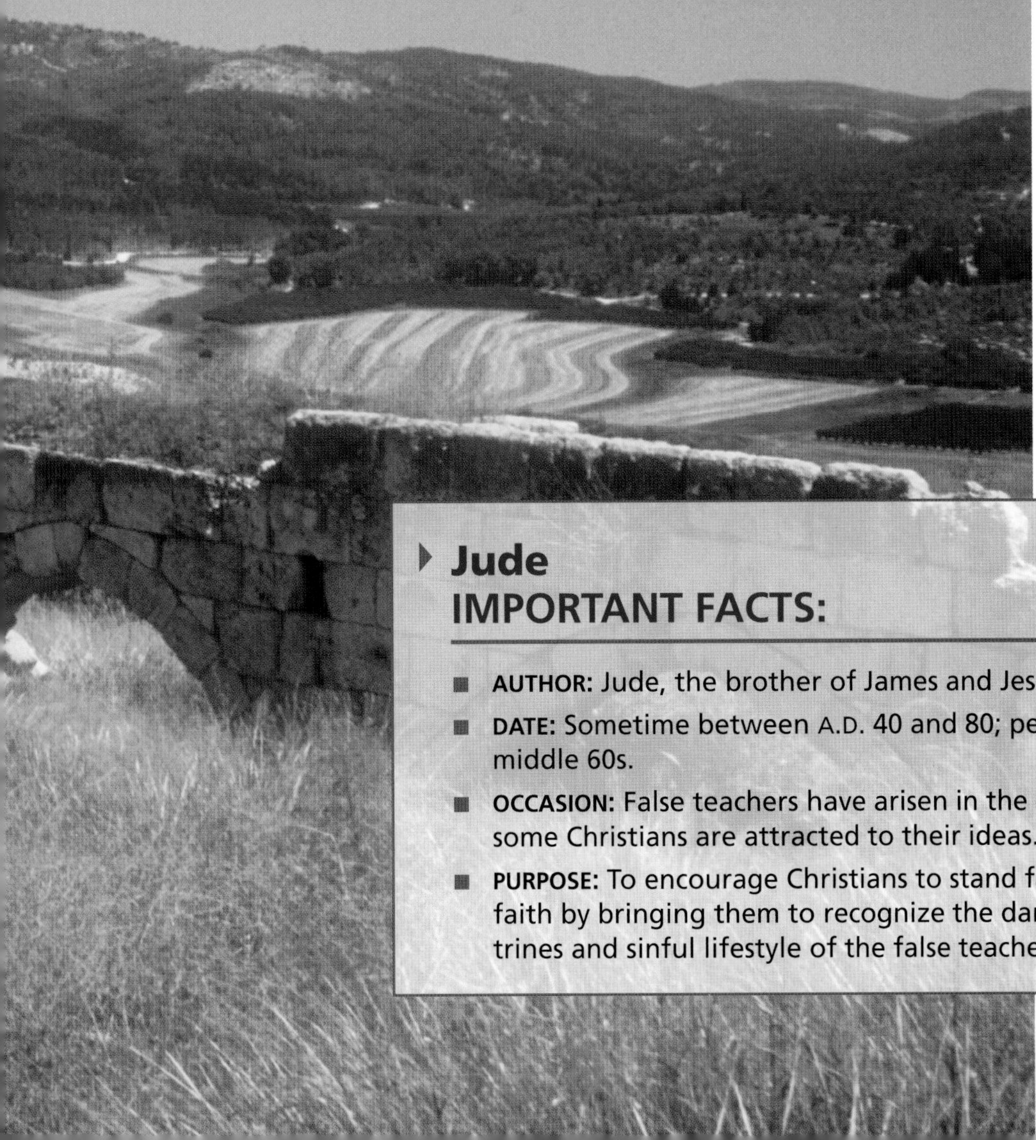

JUDEAN FOOTHILLS WEST OF JERUSALEM

Jude IMPORTANT FACTS:

- **AUTHOR:** Jude, the brother of James and Jesus.
- **DATE:** Sometime between A.D. 40 and 80; perhaps in the middle 60s.
- **OCCASION:** False teachers have arisen in the church, and some Christians are attracted to their ideas.
- **PURPOSE:** To encourage Christians to stand fast in their faith by bringing them to recognize the dangerous doctrines and sinful lifestyle of the false teachers.

The author of this letter is almost certainly Judas, the brother of Jesus, for he identifies himself as a "brother of James." This James must be the famous James who led the Jerusalem church (cf. Acts 15:13–21; 21:18), "the Lord's brother" (Gal. 1:19). Like James in his letter, Jude refrains from claiming to be a brother of the Lord because the physical relationship was the basis neither for his own faith nor for his authority in the church. Jesus' brothers did not believe in his claims during his own lifetime (John 7:3). Only, apparently, after his resurrection did they recognize the truth of his messianic claims and become his followers (Acts 1:14).

With the growth of ascetic traditions of spirituality, Christians in the first centuries began to have difficulties with the idea that Mary did not remain a virgin after the birth of Jesus. They therefore stumbled over references in the New Testament to "brothers" of Jesus. Some, like Jerome, suggested that the word meant "cousins" in these contexts (this interpretation became known as the "Hieronymian" view). But New Testament evidence for this meaning of the word *adelphos* is lacking. Others claimed that Jesus' brothers were sons of Joseph and a wife before Mary (the so-called "Epiphanian" view). Still others see no difficulty in thinking that Mary may have had other children; they think that Jesus' brothers were born to Joseph and Mary after Jesus' birth (the "Helvidian" view).[2]

The Circumstances of the Letter

Jude never appears in any other New Testament book outside the brief mention in Mark 6:3; so we know nothing about his ministry. But Paul's brief allusion to the "Lord's brothers" in 1 Corinthians 9:5 suggests that he may have traveled rather extensively. The lack of specific information about Jude and the very general way he introduces the letter—"to those who are called, who are loved by God the Father and kept by Jesus Christ"—makes it difficult to pinpoint matters such as the date, occasion, or address of the letter

▸ Apocalyptic

An influential movement within Judaism in the time just before and during the New Testament was apocalyptic.[A-1] Scholars debate the exact nature and essence of this movement. But it is commonly agreed that it arose in response to the severe tribulations experienced by the Jewish people in the two centuries before Christ. No tribulation was more traumatic than the attempt of the Seleucid king Antiochus IV "Epiphanes" to eradicate the Jewish religion. His oppression and the resultant successful Jewish guerilla resistance (the Maccabees) took on legendary status among the Jews.

But difficult times did not end for the Jews, as they continued to be subjected to a series of governing powers. Thus, apocalyptic seers tried to make sense of this difficult situation by appealing to knowledge of what God was "really doing" behind the scenes. They claimed to have been given visionary evidence of his true plan and how it would work out in human history.

Apocalyptic literature therefore assured God's struggling people that he was still sovereign and that both judgment for the wicked and deliverance for the righteous would surely come. This message was especially pertinent to the situation Jude was addressing, as he sought to convince his readers of the eventual downfall of the false teachers and to encourage his readers to persevere in their faith in order to attain the final reward.

that he wrote. But the contents of the letter point to "Jewish-Christians living in a Gentile society."[3] Jude's constant reference both to the Old Testament and to Jewish noncanonical books strongly suggests a Jewish audience. But the sins he warns against are those that would typically arise in a Gentile environment. Further, Jude's frequent references to noncanonical Jewish apocalypses, such as *1 Enoch*, suggest that these Jewish-Christians were conversant with this kind of Jewish tradition.

The identity of the false teachers cannot be determined either. Jude's description of them is dominated by condemnation of their licentious lifestyle. They are scornful of authority, greedy, and sexually immoral. Claiming to be leaders of the community, they have nothing of substance to offer in their teaching. Jude's claim that they fulfill the prediction about "scoffers" to come in the last days (vv. 18–19) may suggest that, like the false teachers in 2 Peter, they were skeptical about the return of Christ in glory (see 2 Peter 3:1–7). The profile of the teachers in Jude is therefore so general that identification with any known heretical group in the first century is precarious.

One popular suggestion is that these teachers were gnostics, or (since Gnosticism did not really exist until the second century), "proto-gnostics." Some of the characteristics of the teachers do, indeed, fit what we know of these early gnostic-inclined groups, as we note in the commentary. But the same characteristics fit other groups as well, so we should probably avoid equating the teachers with gnostics. It is more useful to recognize that the false teachers whom Jude condemns represent a certain tendency within the early Christian church: the abuse of God's grace, and the temptation to turn the free offer of forgiveness in Christ into a cloak for sin and a libertine lifestyle (see v. 4).

One other literary matter may help pin down the background of Jude: its relationship to 2 Peter. As the accompanying chart shows, the two letters share common ideas and vocabulary.

Parallels Between Jude and 2 Peter

Jude		2 Peter
4	the false teachers' "condemnation" from the past	2:3
4	they "deny" the "Sovereign [and] Lord"	2:1
6	angels confined for judgment; "gloomy" (2 Peter) and "darkness" (Jude) translate the same Greek word (*zophos*)	2:4
7	Sodom and Gomorrah as examples of judgment of gross evil	2:6
8	they "reject [Jude]/despise [2 Peter] authority" they "slander celestial beings"	2:10
9	angels do not bring "slanderous accusation[s]"	2:11
12	the false teachers are "blemishes"	2:13
12	Jude: "clouds without rain, blown along by the wind" Peter: "springs without water and mists driven by a storm"	2:17
18	"scoffers" following "their own evil [Peter]/ungodly [Jude] desires"	3:3

So close, indeed, are the parallels, that some form of literary relationship must be posited. But scholars disagree about the nature of that relationship. Most think that Peter has borrowed from Jude.[4] Others, however, think that it is just the reverse: Jude borrows from Peter.[5] And still others suggest that both Jude and Peter borrow from a lost common source.[6] We do not have enough evidence to decide the matter. But one intriguing bit of evidence is Jude's reference in vv. 17–18 to a warning from the "apostles" about scoffers that will arise in the last days. Could this be an allusion to 2 Peter 3:3–4?

> First of all, you must understand that in the last days scoffers will come, scoffing and following their own evil desires. They will say, "Where is this 'coming' he promised? Ever since our fathers died, everything goes on as it has since the beginning of creation."

Proof is certainly impossible. But it can be suggested that Jude, facing a similar outbreak of false teaching as did Peter, has borrowed extensively from Peter. Jude would then probably date from about the same time as, or shortly after, 2 Peter—for example, in the middle to late 60s.

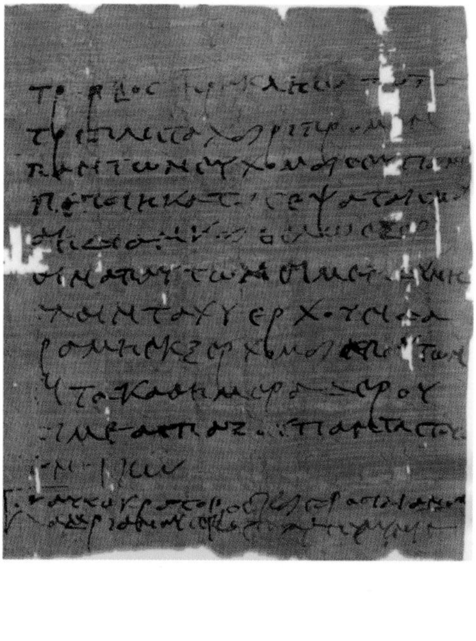

ANCIENT LETTER

A papyrus letter from a son to his father dated to A.D. 127 and found in Egypt.

Jude and Rhetoric

An influential force in ancient Greco-Roman society was the focus on *rhetoric*. We often use this term, or its derivatives, to connote an elaborate, or flowery, manner of speech. But rhetoric in the ancient world was the art of persuasion. Both the Greeks and Romans were fond of legal disputes, and techniques of persuasion were intensely studied and carefully categorized. Aristotle wrote an influential treatise, *The Art of Rhetoric*, on the topic.

F. Duane Watson has persuasively argued that the letter of Jude employs a traditional rhetorical structure.[7] He analyzes the rhetorical movement of the letter as follows, giving each unit the Latin name that had come to be associated with the specific argumentative stage:

- the *exordium* (v. 3): introducing the "case" that the "rhetor" is going to argue
- the *narratio* (v. 4): setting forth the concerns that require the rhetor to address the matter
- the *probatio* (vv. 5–16): seekings to persuade his audience by means of argument and illustration
- the *peroratio* (vv. 17–23): recapitulating the case and appealing to the emotions of the audience in a last-ditch attempt to persuade

Jude, therefore, adopts a strategy of persuasion that fits into the models his world knew. Whether he does so deliberately or unconsciously "echoes" the usual form of argument in his day is hard to determine.

Introduction (1–2)

Jude follows the convention of ancient letters, including New Testament ones, by introducing himself and his readers at the beginning. But he departs from custom in adding a prayer wish for "mercy, peace, and love." His is the only New Testament salutation that does not include a reference to "grace" and the only one to refer to "love."

A servant of Jesus Christ (1). The Greek word here is not *diakonos*, "household servant," but *doulos*, "(bond)-slave." The word, of course, connotes Jude's strong sense of Christ's lordship in his life. But it also implies that his position as Christ's "slave" is an honorable one and one that carries authority. The phrase "servant/slave" of God occurs often in the Old Testament to refer to such revered figures as Moses and David.[8] Note that "Jesus Christ" takes the place of "the Lord" in his honorific title.

A brother of James (1). Why refer to himself as "a brother of James" and *not* indicate that he was a brother of Jesus? We explained the latter in the introduction: Physical relationship to Jesus brought no spiritual benefit or special authority to Jude. But we still must explain why he refers to James. Presumably his readers know and respect James. This, in turn, suggests that Jude writes to Christians living in the areas where James ministered: Jerusalem and surrounding territories.

Those who have been called (1). To be "called" (*klētoi*) means to be summoned by God to enter into his people. The word is not applied to Israel in the Old Testament, but is used in the New Testament regularly to denote believers.

The Occasion and Theme of the Letter (3–4)

As we noted above, these verses correspond to the *narratio* in Jude's rhetorical strategy: the place where he introduces the background and purpose of his argument. Though wanting to write a positive letter of encouragement, Jude must instead mount a sustained attack on people who are abusing God's grace. His goal is to secure the spiritual safety of his readers.

To contend for the faith that was once for all entrusted to the saints (3). "Contend" translates a Greek word (*epagōnizomai*) that refers to athletic contests, such as a wrestling match. Paul reveals this notion in his use of a cognate verb in 1 Corinthians 9:25: "Everyone who *competes* in the games goes into strict training. They do it to get a crown that will not last; but we do it to get a crown that will last forever."[9] The ancient world was as "sports crazy" as ours, so the imagery of athletics would have been a natural one.

The New Testament normally uses the language of "faith" (*pistis*) to describe the subjective response of human beings to Christ: for example, "faith in Christ," "believing in Christ." But sometimes *pistis* refers not so much to the act of believing as that in which one believes. See, for instance, Galatians 1:23: "They only heard the report: 'The man who formerly persecuted us is now preaching the faith he once tried to destroy.'" Jude clearly uses the word in this sense, a meaning underscored by the phrase "once for all entrusted to the saints." The New Testament elsewhere speaks of the basic truth of what God had done in Christ as the "tradition" (*paradosis,* a cognate to the verb here translated "entrusted"). Paul uses the same verb as Jude uses here to talk about his role in "handing down" that tradition (1 Cor. 15:1–8):

Now, brothers, I want to remind you of the gospel I preached to you, which you received and on which you have taken your stand. By this gospel you are saved, if you hold firmly to the word I preached to you. Otherwise, you have believed in vain. For what I received I *passed on to* you as of first importance: that Christ died for our sins according to the Scriptures, that he was buried, that he was raised on the third day according to the Scriptures, and that he appeared to Peter, and then to the Twelve. After that, he appeared to more than five hundred of the brothers at the same time, most of whom are still living, though some have fallen asleep. Then he appeared to James, then to all the apostles, and last of all he appeared to me also, as to one abnormally born.

Paul makes similar references to this tradition (using other language) in 1 Timothy 1:10; 6:3; 2 Timothy 1:13; 4:3; Titus 1:9; 2:1. Jude claims to stand in a line of true teaching about Christ and his significance. Already, in the 60s, a clear notion of "apostolic" teaching had emerged as a standard against which to measure what could be genuinely called Christian and what could not.

Whose condemnation was written about long ago (4). Where exactly was this condemnation predicted? If, as we have suggested, Jude depends on 2 Peter, he may be thinking of Peter's own predictions (see 2 Peter 2:1–4). But "long ago" (*palai*) probably makes a reference to 2 Peter unlikely. Another possibility is that Jude refers to predictions about judgment in *1 Enoch*. He will quote a "prophecy" from this book in Jude 14–16 to document just this point. But we have no good reason, here at the beginning of the letter, to confine Jude's reference to one source. In the course of his argument, he refers to the Old Testament (vv. 5–8, 11), Jewish tradition (vv. 9, 14–16), and the teaching of the apostles (vv. 17–18). Jude has all these in mind in verse 4.

Godless men (4). "Godless" translates *asebeis*, a word that connotes a person who is "without religion," who "fails to worship."[10] A broad term, it can cover all kinds of sins, but Hellenistic Jews used it especially often of irreverence in an eth-

1 Enoch

Jude is clearly fond of the book *1 Enoch*. He quotes it explicitly in Jude 14–15 and is influenced by its teaching at several other places. This book is found in the collection we call the "Pseudepigrapha," a diverse group of Jewish writings from the time just before and after Christ. Like many of the books in this collection, *1 Enoch* is an apocalypse. It purports to be the revelation that Enoch received from God about the spiritual realm and about God's plan for history. Many scholars have studied *1 Enoch* because of its extensive influence on both Jude and other parts of the New Testament. But little agreement has been reached about this book. Most think it was probably written in several stages, with at least some of the sections coming before the time of Christ.[A-2]

The Same Incidents in Jewish Sources		
***Sirach* 16:7–10**	***Damascus Document* 2:17–3:12**	***3 Maccabees* 2:4–7**
"...ancient giants [= angels of Gen. 6] who revolted in their might. He [God] did not spare the neighbors of Lot.... He showed no pity on the doomed nation...."	"The Watchers of the heavens [= angels of Gen. 6] fell ... their males [of the people of God] were cut off in the wilderness."	"You destroyed ... the giants.... You consumed with fire and sulfur the people of Sodom."
***Testament of Naphtali* 3:4–5**	**Mishnah, *Sanhedrin* 10:3**	
"... so that you do not become like Sodom, which departed from the order of nature. Likewise the Watchers departed from nature's order...."	"The men of Sodom have no share in the world to come.... The generation of the wilderness have no share in the world to come."	

ical sense: "not theoretical atheism, but practical godlessness."[11] This is probably Jude's intention too, since he says little about the false teachers' doctrinal errors and much about their aberrant lifestyle.

Certain men ... secretly ... godless ... immorality (4). We should briefly note the way Jude uses strong negative and emotive language to introduce these false teachers. He is clearly already engaged in his argument to convince his Christian readers to have nothing to do with such people.

Condemnation of the False Teachers: Cycle 1 (5–10)

In verses 5–16, Jude runs through three "cycles" in his condemnation of the false teachers. In each (vv. 5–10, 11–13, 14–16), he cites Old Testament or early Christian creedal traditions and then applies them to the false teachers (using the word "these," vv. 8, 12, 16). Verses 5–10 focus on prominent Old Testament illustrations of judgment, but also include an allusion to a Jewish tradition. But Jude may be somewhat dependent on Jewish traditions even in his use of Old Testament material, for the same incidents that he cites in verses 5–7 are also found together in several Jewish sources (see table above).

I want to remind you (5). Ancient letter writers made the transition from the introduction to the body by means of a "disclosure formula," such as "But I want you to know," or "But let me remind you."

The Lord delivered his people out of Egypt (5). Jude, of course, alludes to one of the great formative events in Israel's history: God's rescuing his people from their slavery in Egypt in order to form them into his own special people (Ex. 6–14). An interesting variant reading in some manuscripts has "*Jesus* delivered his people out of Egypt" in place of "Lord." A few scholars think this may be original, reflecting the same tradition that Paul refers to in 1 Corinthians 10:4, where he identifies the "rock" that followed the Israelites in the desert with Christ. But the variant does not have sufficient support for it to be considered original.

Later destroyed those who did not believe (5). The generation God rescued from Egypt doubted God's power and promise in the desert. They were therefore sentenced to die in that desert and did not enter the Promised Land (e.g., Num. 14).

Angels who did not keep their positions of authority (6). Jude's first and third examples of judgment are well-known to any reader of the Old Testament. But who are these "angels" who sinned and were sentenced to hell? Some commentators think this refers to the primeval "fall" of Satan and his minions, a tradition that some think is alluded to in Isaiah 14 and Ezekiel 28. But, as we noted in the introduction to this section, Jude seems to be following here a pattern of references found elsewhere in Judaism, which included reference to a widespread Jewish tradition based on Genesis 6:1–4:

When men began to increase in number on the earth and daughters were born to them, the sons of God saw that the daughters of men were beautiful, and they married any of them they chose. Then the LORD said, "My Spirit will not contend with man forever, for he is mortal; his days will be a hundred and twenty years." The Nephilim were on the earth in those days—and also afterward—when the sons of God went to the daughters of men and had children by them. They were the heroes of old, men of renown.

Old Testament scholars debate over whether these "sons of God" were men or angels. But Jewish tradition seemed pretty clearly to come down on the side of angels. This text, in fact, became the basis for a common explanation of the origin of sin among Jewish apocalyptic writers in particular: The angels, often called "watchers," introduced evil into the world by cohabiting with human women. See, for instance, *1 Enoch* 6:1–2:[12]

In those days, when the children of man had multiplied, it happened that there were born unto them handsome and beautiful daughters. And the angels, the children of heaven, saw them and desired them, and they said to one another, "Come, let us choose wives for ourselves from among the daughters of man and beget us children."

Kept in darkness, bound with everlasting chains (6). Jude here uses common ancient images of divine judgment. "Darkness" was associated with the place of the dead in Greek thought in conjunction with the idea of the underworld. This language, along with reference to "chains," is picked up in what seems to have been a favorite Jewish book of Jude, *1 Enoch*. Note *1 Enoch* 10:4–6:

And secondly the Lord said to Raphael, "Bind Azazel hand and foot and throw him into the darkness!" And he made a hole in the desert which was in Dudael and cast him there; he threw on top of him rugged and sharp rocks. And he covered his face in order that he might not see the light; and in order that he might be sent into the fire on the great day of judgment.

Sodom and Gomorrah and the surrounding towns (7). See Genesis 19:20–22, Deuteronomy 29:23; where reference is made to Admah, Zeboiim, and Zoar.

Perversion (7). This is the NIV rendering of a difficult phrase in Greek, literally translated "going after other flesh." Since homosexuality figures prominently in the stories about Sodom and Gomorrah, most interpreters think that "other flesh" refers to the tendency to have sexual relationships with "flesh" other than that which God had ordained. But a few interpreters think that the reference may be to the "flesh" of angels. This view is not as far-fetched as it might at first appear, since Jewish tradition associated the sin of the angels (v. 6) with that of the people in Sodom and Gomorrah. As the angels sinned by yearning for human flesh, so the people in Sodom and Gomorrah erred by seeking angelic flesh. But it seems unlikely that Jude associates "flesh" with angels. Thus, the usual view, that Jude refers to homosexuality, is to be preferred.

They serve as an example of those who suffer the punishment of eternal fire (7). God's judgment on the cities was spectacular and final. According to Genesis 19:24, "the LORD rained down burning sulfur on Sodom and Gomorrah—from the LORD out of the heavens." Contemporaries of Jude saw in the barren topography of the area traditionally associated with the cities continuing reminders of the judgment of God. See, for example, Philo: "Even to this day there are seen in Syria monuments of the unprecedented destruction that fell upon them, in the ruins, and ashes, and sulphur, and smoke, and dusky flame which still is sent up from the ground as of a fire smouldering beneath" (Philo, *Moses* 2.56). "Fire" was a common metaphor for judgment.[13]

These dreamers (8). As Jude turns now to apply his illustrations to the false teachers, he first calls them "dreamers." This word refers to visionary experiences in its one other New Testament occurrence (Acts 2:17, quoting Joel 2:28). The same verb is used in the LXX to refer to the visions that false prophets claimed to receive (e.g., Deut. 13:2, 4, 6).

[They] reject authority (8). The word "authority" (*kyriotēs*) comes from the same word root as the word for "Lord" (*kyrios*). Jude probably means these false teachers are rejecting the lordship of Christ.

Slander celestial beings (8). "Celestial beings" is probably the correct interpretation of the Greek here, which has simply "glories" (*doxai*). Glory was frequently associated with angels in Jewish teaching. How were the false teachers "slandering" (or "blaspheming") angels? Some interpreters, who think that the false teachers had some kind of relationship to Gnosticism, cite evidence that gnostics spoke against angels by associating them with an inferior god. But the link to Gnosticism is not that clear. Thus, the connection may be with the false teachers' skepticism about future judgment. This skepticism is explicitly mentioned in the parallel 2 Peter 3 and may be hinted at in Jude 18 ("scoffers"). Jewish tradition saw the angels as having a critical role in the judgment. Another possibility is that Jude is referring to the false teachers' immorality. For angels were considered to be the guardians of the law (cf. Acts 7:38; Gal. 3:19–20), and by flaunting the law, the false teachers may also, effectively, have been slandering angels.

But perhaps we should look in a different direction entirely. The connection between Jude 8 and 9 suggests that the "celestial beings" may be evil rather than good angels. If this is the case, the false teachers may have been pooh-poohing any baneful influence from these evil angels.

The archangel Michael (9). Jews in the intertestamental period had a fascination with angels, speculating about their significance and constructing elaborate hierachies of relationships. The "archangel" was the highest rank. Jews sometimes named four, sometimes seven, archangels. Michael, mentioned three times in the Old Testament (Dan. 10:13, 21; 12:1) and once in the New Testament (Rev. 12:7) is always included in this rank and is often singled out as the most prominent of the archangels.

When he was disputing with the devil about the body of Moses (9). This story appears neither in the Old Testament nor in any extant Jewish book. But several early Christian fathers claim that the story appeared in a book known to them, called variously *The Assumption of Moses* or *The Testament of Moses.*[14] In any case, the story seems to be based loosely on Zechariah 3:1–2 (see quotation of this passage in comments on Jude 23). We have no way of knowing what status Jude accorded this story about the body of Moses. Did he think that the incident actually took place? Or does he simply view it as a well-known tradition that he can cite to make his point—similar to a contemporary preacher's citing an incident from *The Chronicles of Narnia?*

> **REFLECTIONS**
>
> **MOST PEOPLE LIKE TO FOCUS ON THE POSITIVE.** Christians are no exception. We like to bask in the good news of all the blessings God has showered on us. This positive emphasis was what Jude had been hoping to convey in his letter (v. 3). But circumstances demanded otherwise. False teachers were such a threat that he felt compelled to warn his readers about them. Those of us in Christian ministry will often find ourselves in similar situations. We would rather not dwell on the negative; and we do not want to be thought "unchristian" by criticizing others who claim the name of the Lord. But Jude's letter stands as an example of the need for negative preaching on occasion. God's people need to be warned about the dangerous heresies that pop up all over the place in our day. The faithful teacher of God's Word will need to help people discern truth from error.

Condemnation of the False Teachers: Cycle 2 (11–13)

In his second round of condemnations, Jude associates the false teachers with three notorious Old Testament sinners and then describes their immoral and reckless lifestyle.

Woe to them! (11). The English "woe" transliterates the Greek *ouai,* which in turn translates a Hebrew word used often by the prophets to warn about the pain and distress that the judgment would bring. See, for example, Isaiah 3:11: "Woe to the wicked! Disaster is upon them! They will be paid back for what their hands have done."

The way of Cain (11). In the Old Testament Cain is known especially as the first murderer.[15] The false teachers may then, Jude implies, be "murdering" the souls of people through their destructive heresies. But Jewish tradition suggests other options. Some texts picture Cain as the classic example of an ungodly skeptic. The Jerusalem Targum, an Aramaic paraphrase of the Pentateuch, presents Cain as saying, "There is no judgment, no judge, no future life; no reward will be given to the righteous, and no judgment will be imposed on the wicked."[16] Other texts claim that Cain was a corrupter of humankind. Josephus, for instance, writes that Cain "incited to luxury and pillage all whom he met, and became their instructor in wicked practices."[17]

Balaam's error (11). As Jude implies in this context, Balaam, the pagan prophet whom king Balak hired to curse Israel (Num. 22–24), was know above all for his greed.[18]

Korah's rebellion (11). Korah "became insolent and rose up against Moses" (Num. 16:1–2) and led two hundred other prominent Israelites in rebellion against Moses and the Lord. God reacted with a severe judgment, causing the earth to open up and swallow all the rebels along with their households. Numbers 16 also mentions judgment by fire, as does a later commentary on the incident (Ps. 106:16–18). Even in Moses' day, Korah became a warning example to those who might be tempted to resist the Lord and his appointed leaders (cf. Num. 26:9–10). The vivid nature of this incident captured the imagination of later Jews. Korah became the poster boy for the antinomian heretic.[19]

Blemishes (12). The word (*spilades*) should probably be translated "(hidden) reef" (see NASB). Jude pictures the false teachers as lying in wait, like reefs below the surface of the water, to bring destruction on believers.

Love feasts (12). Early Christians ate a festive meal together when they celebrated the Lord's Supper. The practice is attested in many ancient Christian texts and is assumed in 1 Corinthians 11:17–32.[20]

Shepherds who feed only themselves (12). "Shepherds" is not a metaphor here, as if Jude suggests the false teachers are like actual shepherds. He uses the word in the technical sense it gained in the Old Testament and Judaism, as a way of denoting the leaders of God's people. Jude may be thinking here specifically of Ezekiel 34:2: "Son of man, prophesy against the shepherds of Israel; prophesy and say to them: 'This is what the Sovereign LORD says: Woe to the shepherds of Israel who only take care of themselves! Should not shepherds take care of the flock?'"

Clouds without rain (12). The image is a natural one for people who promise what they will not, or cannot, deliver. See Proverbs 25:14: "Like clouds and wind without rain is a man who boasts of gifts he does not give."

Autumn trees, without fruit and uprooted—twice dead (12). A tree without fruit in the autumn has not fulfilled its purpose in being. Jude's imagery in this context may again be dependent on a tradition preserved in *1 Enoch* 80:2–3:

> In respect to their days, the sinners and the winter are cut short. Their seed shall lag behind in their lands and in their fertile fields, and in all their activities upon the earth. He will turn and appear in their time, and withhold rain; and the sky shall stand still at that time. Then the vegetable shall slacken and not grow in its season, and the fruit shall not be born in its proper season.

Wild waves of the sea (13). Jude may be thinking of Isaiah 57:20: "But the wicked are like the tossing sea, which cannot rest, whose waves cast up mire and mud."

Wandering stars (13). The Greek word for "wander" (*planaō*) is the word from which we get our word "planet." The ancients sought to find harmony and sense in the movement of the heavenly bodies and were therefore puzzled and offended at the arbitrary movements of the planets. They therefore sometimes attributed their movements to the influence of evil angels. Note *1 Enoch* 18:13–15:

> And I saw the seven stars (which) were like great, burning moutains. (Then) the angel said (to me), "This is the (ultimate) end of heaven and earth: it is the prison house for the stars and the powers of heaven. And the stars which roll over upon the fire, they are the ones which have transgressed the commandments of God from the beginning of their rising because they did not arrive punctually."

Whether by chance or not, the four images Jude uses in verses 12b–13—clouds, trees, waves, planets—correspond to the typical ancient division of the four "regions" of the earth: air, earth, sea, and the heavens.

Condemnation of the False Teachers: Cycle 3 (14–16)

Jude's final denunciation of the false teachers uses a long quotation from *1 Enoch*. He uses the quotation to confirm the pronouncement of judgment on these false teachers.

Enoch, the seventh from Adam (14). Enoch, an early descendant of Adam through the line of Seth, appears in the Old Testament only in genealogical lists (Gen. 5:18–24; 1 Chron. 1:3). But interest among Jews was focused on him because of the scriptural claim that he "walked with God; then he was no more, because God took him away" (Gen. 5:24). The text suggests that, like Elijah (2 Kings 2:1–13), Enoch did not die but was translated directly to heaven (see also Heb. 11:5). Enoch's enigmatic appearance in the Old Testament made him a natural figure for Jewish speculation; and at least two books of apocalyptic visions were written in his name.

He can be called the "seventh" from Adam because Jews counted inclusively (i.e., including the first and last in a series): Adam, Seth, Enosh, Kenan, Mahalalel, Jared, Enoch. Jewish writers dwell on the same point (*Jub.* 7:39), presumably because seven was the number that symbolized perfection.

"See, the Lord is coming . . ." (14b–15). The quotation comes from *1 Enoch* 1:9:

> Behold, he will arrive with ten millions of the holy ones in order to execute judgment upon all. He will destroy the wicked ones and censure all flesh on account of everything that they have done, that which the sinners and the wicked ones committed against him.

Absent from this text is Jude's language about "harsh words ungodly sinners have spoken against" the Lord. Jude may add this reference from *1 Enoch*, 27:2: "This accursed valley is for those accursed forever; here will gather together all (those) accursed ones, those who speak with their mouth unbecoming words against the Lord and utter hard words concerning his glory."

Grumblers (16). This language occurs regularly in the Old Testament to depict Israelites who grumbled against God for bringing them out of Egypt into the barren desert.[21] So Jude may imply that the false teachers are also grumbling against God.

The Need to Persevere (17–23)

As we suggested in the introduction, this section of Jude's letter corresponds to the *peroratio* in a rhetorical arrangement: the appeal to the emotions to seal the orator's case. Typical of this rhetorical style,

Jude repeats some of the key ideas from the beginning of the argument:

- "love": vv. 1 and 2; cf. "beloved" in v. 3/"keep yourselves in God's love" (v. 21)
- "mercy": v. 2/"be merciful to those who doubt" (v. 22)
- "keep": "kept by Jesus Christ" (v. 1)/"keep yourselves in God's love" (v. 21)
- The need to adhere to apostolic tradition: "contend for the faith that was once for all entrusted to the saints" (v. 3)/"remember what the apostles of our Lord Jesus Christ foretold" (v. 17)
- Identification and negative characterization of the false teachers: v. 4/vv. 18–19.

Jude wants his readers to avoid the contagion of the false teaching by taking to heart the teaching of the apostles (vv. 17–19) and by striving to maintain their own spiritual vitality (vv. 20–21), and to minister to those who are affected by the false teaching (vv. 22–23).

Scoffers (18). If Jude is dependent on 2 Peter 3:3 (see the introduction), he is probably assuming that the scoffing is directed toward predictions of the Lord's coming back in glory. But it is also possible, especially considering the degree to which Jude faults the teachers for ethical lapses, that he is thinking of their scoffing at commandments that require them to lead righteous lives.

The men who divide you (19). The verb Jude uses here (*apodiorizō*) is rare. Because Aristotle uses the verb to mean "make logical distinctions," it has been supposed that Jude is referring to the gnostic tendency to divide believers into two distinct categories, based on their ability to apprehend esoteric spiritual truth. But we must again note that the association of the false teachers with gnostics is anything but certain. Perhaps

▸ *1 Enoch* and the Canon of Scripture

Jude's explicit quotation from a noncanonical book has naturally been the subject of much comment when it comes to the issue of the canon. Early Christians took three different positions on the significance of the quotation for the canon:

1. A few fathers argued on the basis of Jude that *1 Enoch* should be included in the canon (e.g., Clement of Alexandria, *Eccl. Proph.* 3; Tertullian, *De cultu fem.* 1.3).
2. Other fathers took the opposite tack: Because Jude quotes from *1 Enoch,* it should be excluded from the canon (Jerome refers to these in *De. vir. ill.* 4).
3. Augustine thought that Jude's quotation proved that *1 Enoch* was inspired at some points only (*City of God* 15.23).

Modern opinion is likewise divided. Some scholars think that Jude reveals that the canon of Scripture was still "open" at that time and that we should therefore be wary of the whole idea of canon. But most interpreters rightly note that Jude never calls *1 Enoch* "Scripture" (*graphē*). While using the book in his letter, he never accords it canonical status. It remains an open question just how Jude viewed the actual words that he quotes. He may have simply reported these words as a known tradition without implying anything about their divine origin or authority. But his use of the verb "prophesy" suggests perhaps that he did think that *1 Enoch* included at this point a genuine prophecy from Enoch.

Jude simply means that the false teachers, as false teachers usually do, are creating dissension in the community.

Keep yourselves in God's love (21). Jude may be thinking of the teaching of Jesus: "Now remain in my love" (John 15:9). The allusion would be particularly appropriate, since Jesus goes on to indicate that obeying his commandments is one key manifestation of love.

Be merciful to those who doubt (22). According to the NIV, Jude urges his readers to take specific action toward three different groups in verses 22–23. The NIV is probably right in this decision, but we should note that the text is complicated, both from a textual-critical standpoint and from a grammatical standpoint (note the different arrangement in KJV; TEV; RSV). "Those who doubt" likely refers to believers who are wavering in their commitment, somewhat attracted to the false teaching but not yet ready to follow it all the way.

Snatch others from the fire and save them (23). Other believers have gone much farther down the road of the false teaching; so far that they are in danger of eternal damnation ("fire"). Jude's imagery reflects Zechariah 3:1–4:

> Then he showed me Joshua the high priest standing before the angel of the LORD, and Satan standing at his right side to accuse him. The LORD said to Satan, "The LORD rebuke you, Satan! The LORD, who has chosen Jerusalem, rebuke you! Is not this man a burning stick snatched from the fire?" Now Joshua was dressed in filthy clothes as he stood before the angel. The angel said to those who were standing before him, "Take off his filthy clothes." Then he said to Joshua, "See, I have taken away your sin, and I will put rich garments on you."

To others show mercy, mixed with fear—hating even the clothing stained by corrupted flesh (23). Jude continues to use imagery from Zechariah 3. The word "stained" comes from the same verb (*spiloō*) that occurs in Zechariah 3:3 to describe the clothes ("filthy") that Joshua is to take off. Jude is probably now thinking of the false teachers themselves. They are to be shown mercy in the prayers of the community for them.

Doxology (24–25)

Jude concludes his letter with one of the greatest ascriptions of glory to God that we find in the Bible.

Without fault (24). The Greek word (*amōmos*) originally was applied to sacrifices (cf. Heb. 9:14; 1 Peter 1:19), but was transferred into the moral realm.

The only God (25). Pursuing the idea that Gnosticism may lurk in the background of Jude, some scholars think that Jude makes this point to counteract their typical emphasis on the existence of two or more competing gods. But the ascription is so common in Judaism that this particular background need not be considered.

ANNOTATED BIBLIOGRAPHY

Bauckham, Richard. *Jude, 2 Peter*. WBC. Waco, Tex.: Word, 1983.

The most important conservative commentary on these letters in decades; arguably the best technical commentary now available. Rich in references to extrabiblical materials and marred only by its assumption of pseudonymity for 2 Peter.

Bigg, Charles. *A Critical and Exegetical Commentary on the Epistles of St. Peter and St. Jude*. ICC. New York: Scribners, 1903.

Classic treatment, oriented to historical and grammatical issues.

Kelly, J. N. D. *A Commentary on the Epistles of Peter and of Jude*. HNTC. New York: Harper & Row, 1969.

Careful treatment of the text.

Mayor, Joseph B. *The Epistle of St. Jude and the Second Epistle of St. Peter: Greek Text with Introduction, Notes and Comments*. Grand Rapids: Baker, 1979 (= 1907).

Lengthy treatment, focusing especially on historical and linguistic matters.

Moo, Douglas J. *2 Peter and Jude*. NIVAC. Grand Rapids: Zondervan, 1996.

Exposition of the English text with focus on contemporary application.

Neyrey, Jerome H. *2 Peter, Jude: A New Translation with Introduction and Commentary*. AB. Garden City, N.Y.: Doubleday, 1993.

The most recent English language technical commentary, incorporating social-critical and literary approaches.

CHAPTER NOTES

Main Text Notes

1. Acts 5:37; Luke 6:16; Acts 1:13; Acts 15:22; cf. 15:27, 32; Mark 6:3.
2. For a recent survey of the whole matter, see esp. R. Bauckham, *Jude and the Relatives of Jesus in the Early Church* (Edinburgh: T. & T. Clark, 1990).
3. R. Bauckham, *Jude, 2 Peter* (WBC; Waco, Tex.: Word, 1983), 16.
4. E.g., Bauckham, *Jude, 2 Peter,* 141–43.
5. E.g., C. A. Bigg, *A Critical and Exegetical Commentary on the Epistles of St. Peter and St. Jude* (ICC; New York: Scribners, 1903), 216–24.
6. E. M. B. Green, *The Second Epistle of Peter and the Epistle of Jude* (TNTC; Grand Rapids: Eerdmans, 1968), 50–55.
7. F. D. Watson, *Invention, Arrangement, and Style: Rhetorical Criticism of Jude and 2 Peter* (SBLDS 104; Atlanta: Scholars, 1988).
8. Josh. 14:7; 2 Kings 18:12; Ps. 18:1; Ezek. 34:23.
9. See also Col. 1:29; 1 Tim. 4:10; 6:12; 2 Tim. 4:7.
10. See Rom. 5:6; 1 Tim. 1:9; 1 Peter 4:18; 2 Peter 2:5–6; 3:7.
11. Bauckham, *Jude, 2 Peter,* 35–36.
12. See also *Jub.* 5:1; 10:1–6; Josephus, *Ant.* 1.73; Philo, *Giants* 6; QG 1.92; CD 2:18.
13. See, e.g., Ps. 18:7–8; 1QS 2:8; 4:13.
14. Scholars dispute the relationship of these two books and/or titles (see discussion in Bauckham, *Jude, 2 Peter,* 65–76).
15. Gen. 4:1–16; cf. 1 John 3:12.
16. See *Targum Pseudo-Jonathan* on Num. 16:1–2.
17. Josephus, *Ant.* 1.2.2 §61; see also Philo, *Posterity* 38–39.
18. See Targum on Num. 22–24; Philo, *Moses* 1.266–28; *Migration* 114; Rev. 2:14.
19. See Josephus, *Ant.* 4.2.2–3 §§14–21.
20. See G. Wainwright, "Lord's Supper, Love Feast," *DLNT*, 686–94.
21. E.g., Ex. 16:7–12; 17:3; Num. 14:27–29; 17:5, 10.

Sidebar and Chart Notes

A-1. For further information on apocalyptic, see L. J. Kreitzer, "Apocalyptic, Apocalypticism," *DLNT*, 55–68; for more detail, P. D. Hanson, *The Dawn of Apocalyptic* (Philadelphia: Fortress, 1975); Christopher Rowland, *The Open Heaven: A Study of Apocalyptic in Judaism and Christianity* (New York: Crossroad, 1982); D. S. Russell, *The Method and Message of Jewish Apocalyptic* (Philadelphia: Westminster, 1964).

A-2. For further information on *1 En.*, see *OTP*, 1:5–12.

CREDITS FOR PHOTOS AND MAPS

Arnold, Clinton E.	pp. 14, 60, 62, 90
Bredow, Dennis	p. 61
Dunn, Cheryl (for Talbot Bible Lands)	pp. 97, 100
Haradine, Jane (public domain photos)	pp. 30, 64, 71
Isachar, Hanan	p. 107
King, Jay	p. 17
Kohlenberger, John R. III	pp. 4, 6, 36, 60
Konstas, Ioannis	pp. 23, 48, 68, 99
Radovan, Zev	pp. 16, 18, 72, 80, 106
Ritmeyer, Leen	p. 84
Tabernacle	p. 69
University of Michigan	p. 114
Wilson, Mark	pp. 2–3, 5, 7
Zondervan Image Archive (Neal Bierling)	pp. 9, 29, 34–35, 38, 42, 44(2), 46(2), 58–59, 66, 82, 87, 94–95, 102–3, 110–11

ALSO AVAILABLE

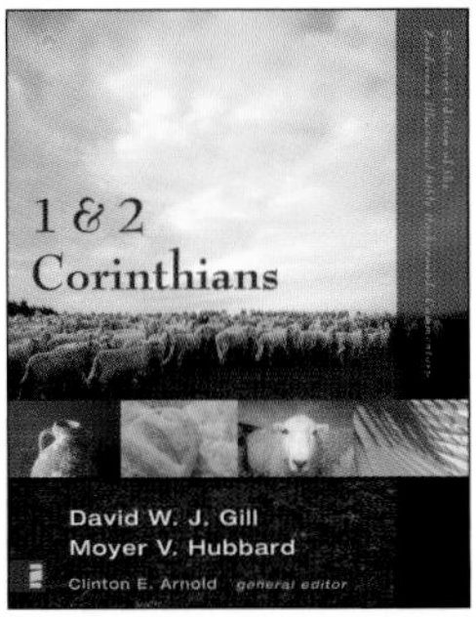

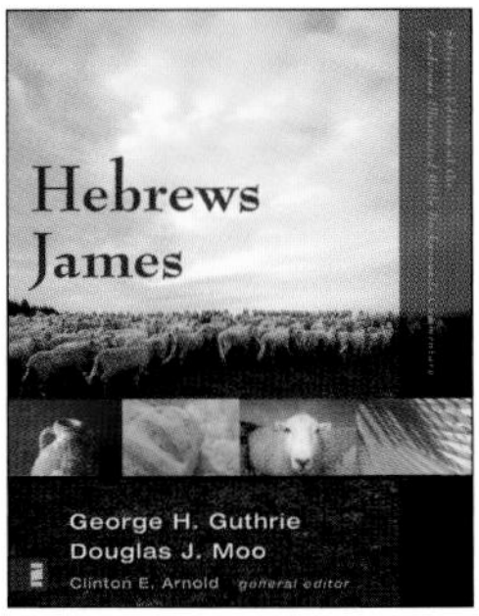